CAPITALISM
AND THE JEWS

CAPITALISM
AND THE JEWS

JERRY Z. MULLER

PRINCETON UNIVERSITY PRESS   PRINCETON AND OXFORD

Copyright © 2010 by Princeton University Press
Published by Princeton University Press, 41 William
Street, Princeton, New Jersey 08540
In the United Kingdom: Princeton University Press, 6
Oxford Street, Woodstock, Oxfordshire OX20 1TW

All Rights Reserved

Library of Congress Cataloging-in-Publication Data

Muller, Jerry Z., 1954–
    Capitalism and the Jews / Jerry Z. Muller.
        p. cm.
    Includes bibliographical references and index.
    ISBN 978-0-691-14478-8 (hardcover : alk.
paper) 1. Capitalism. 2. Jews—History. 3. Jewish
businesspeople. 4. Communism. 5. Nationalism.
I. Title.
    HB501.M825 2010
    330.940089'924—c22   2009027147

British Library Cataloging-in-Publication Data is available

This book has been composed in Janson text
Printed on acid-free paper. ∞
press.princeton.edu
Printed in the United States of America

10 9 8 7 6 5 4 3 2

For

STEVEN E. ASCHHEIM & STEPHEN J. WHITFIELD

dear friends and colleagues

CONTENTS

CAPITALISM
AND THE JEWS

INTRODUCTION

Thinking about Jews and Capitalism

Capitalism has been the most important force in shaping the fate of the Jews in the modern world. Of course, one could plausibly argue that it has been the most important force in shaping the fate of *everyone* in the modern world. But Jews have had a special relationship with capitalism, for they have been particularly good at it. Not all of them, of course. But, whenever they have been allowed to compete on an equal legal footing, they have tended to do disproportionately well. This has been a blessing—and a curse.

Jews have been a conspicuous presence in the history of capitalism, both as symbol and as reality. Yet the relationship of the Jews to capitalism has received less attention than its significance merits.[1] One reason for this relative neglect is no doubt the division of labor characteristic of modern academic research. Academic historians tend to focus on the history of a particular nation or region—while Jews were scattered across national and regional boundaries. The encounter of the Jews with capitalism confounds disciplinary boundaries as well: it is the stuff of economic history as well as of social history, of political history as well as cultural history, of the history of business, but also of the family and the nation-state. But there are other reasons for the relative neglect of the topic as well. Discussions of Jews and capitalism touch upon neuralgic subjects.

For Jews, Jewish economic success has long been a source of both pride and embarrassment. For centuries, Jewish economic success led anti-Semites to condemn capitalism as a form of Jewish domination and exploitation, or to attribute Jewish success to unsavory qualities of the Jews themselves. The anti-Semitic context of such discussions led Jews to downplay the reality of their economic achievement—except in internal conversations. Moreover, for most people, the workings of advanced capitalist economies are opaque and difficult to comprehend. When economic times are bad and people are hurting, some inevitably search for a more easily grasped, concrete target on which to pin their ill fortunes. That target has often been the Jews. Even today, some Jews regard the public discussion of Jews and capitalism as intrinsically impolitic, as if conspiratorial fantasies about Jews and money can be eliminated by prudent silence.

For economists and economic historians, the extent to which modern capitalism has been shaped by premodern cultural conceptions and cultural predispositions is a source of puzzlement at best. It simply doesn't fit into the categories in which contemporary economic historians who have adopted the armature of econometrics are predisposed to think. In recent decades, economists have added the concept of "human capital" to their kitbag, by which they mean the characteristics that make for economic success. But they prefer to think of it in terms of measurable criteria such as years of schooling. To the extent that human capital involves character traits and varieties of know-how that are not provided by formal education, it becomes methodologically elusive. Much of the reality of economic history, and of the Jewish role within it, is bound to elude those who proceed on the tacit premise that "if you can't count it, it doesn't count."

For liberals, the reality of differential group achievement under conditions of legal equality is something of a scandal, an affront to egalitarian assumptions. For it casts a shadow of doubt on the shibboleth of "equality of opportunity." If it turns out that the ability to take advantage of opportunity is deeply influenced by cultural traits transmitted in the private realm of the family and the cultural community, then inequality of outcome cannot be attributed merely to legal discrimination, nor can it be eliminated by formal, public institutions, such as schools.

For nationalists, the fact that modern nationalism had fateful consequences for the Jews precisely because the Jews were so *good* at capitalism was itself a source of embarrassment. In the late nineteenth and twentieth centuries, many nationalist movements sought to restrict Jewish citizenship and legal equality out of the perception (partly founded) that Jews excelled at capitalist activity compared to their non-Jewish countrymen. For many nationalists, in countries from prerevolutionary Russia, to Poland, Hungary, and Germany, the "real" nation was defined in good part over-and-against the Jews. When economic life was conceived of as a zero-sum game, in which the gains of some could only come at the expense of others, the gains of the Jews were made responsible for the psychic or material pains of the "authentic" members of the nation. The extent to which the fellow feeling between gentry, artisans, peasants, and industrial workers was forged in a shared and cultivated antipathy to the Jewish "other" is a part of national history that nationalists would rather forget.

For all these reasons, the exploration of Jews and capitalism has tended to be left to apologists, ideologues, and anti-Semites. This book, by contrast, tries to make sense of patterns in modern history that tend to be neglected by social scientists.

Jews were associated with trade and with the lending of money long before the rise of a recognizably modern capitalism in the seventeenth century. That association would have ongoing effects. It helps to account for the fact of disproportionate Jewish success under conditions of modern capitalism. In addition, the way in which modern, non-Jewish intellectuals thought about capitalism was often related to how they thought about Jews. Those evaluations in turn affected the ways in which Jews thought about *themselves*, about their economic role and their position in society. Jewish intellectuals such as Moses Mendelssohn were well aware of this connection, and linked their case for civil equality for the Jews with arguments about the positive function of the economic activities in which Jews were engaged.

Yet the disproportionate economic success of the Jews made them a lightning rod for the discontent and resentment that was almost everywhere a product of what Joseph Schumpeter called the "creative destruction" that was part and parcel of capitalist dynamism. By that he meant the displacement of older forms of production, consumption, and styles of life by new forms, created by capitalist innovation. Added to this source of animus was the fact that the development of capitalism went hand in hand with the rise of the modern nation-state, which, in much of the Old World, took the form of an ethnic nationalism that defined Jews as outside the national community. That led to new, more modern forms of anti-Jewish animus, rooted less in religious difference than in the resentment of Jewish economic success. And that in turn led a small but salient minority of Jews to embrace Communism, the most radical form of anticapitalism. That embrace had fateful consequences of its own. And finally, it led a growing portion of Jewry to conclude that in an age of capitalism and nationalism, Jews needed a nation-state of their own.

Thus the interlocking themes of the four essays that make up this book, which traverse the boundary between general and Jewish history, and between intellectual, economic, and political history. They aim to show the relevance of the experience of the Jews to the larger themes of modern European history: of the development of capitalism, Communism, nationalism, and fascism. And while focused on modern Europe, they also deal with the effects of these phenomena beyond Europe, including the United States and Israel.

When social scientists set out to explain the relationship of the Jews to capitalism, they frequently make use of the notion of Jews as a "diasporic merchant minority." That concept provides an indispensable though ultimately unsatisfactory framework for understanding the relationship between Jews and modern capitalism.[2] Since their dispersion from the Land of Israel—a dispersion that began when the Jews still had a sovereign state—Jews have lived as a diaspora, a minority in the Roman Empire, then in Christian Europe and in the lands of Islam. Though by no means a merchant people for much of their history, they became one in medieval Christendom. Like other diasporic merchant minorities—the Armenians, or the Greeks, or overseas Chinese—they developed transregional trading networks, as well as the skills and cultural dispositions conducive to trade. Such minorities are characterized by the combination of specialized economic competence and political powerlessness.

Yet the category of diasporic merchant minority is by itself inadequate to grasp the significance of the Jews in Christian Europe. For the Jews were permitted to engage in otherwise stigmatized economic activities, especially the lending of money at interest, because of their peculiar place in Christian theology. As the community from which Christ sprang, they were to be tolerated. In Christian eyes, it was the narrative of the Old Testament that provided the warrant for Jesus' role in the scheme of salvation. The Jews, as the people of the Old Testament, were to survive to provide tangible evidence of the historical depth of the Christian narrative, and eventually to provide testimony at the second coming of Christ. But the failure of the Jews to recognize Jesus as God was a testament to their blindness, their spiritual malformation. According to Augustine and later Christian theologians, Jews were to be tolerated in Christian Europe—as those of other faiths were not. But their status had to be sufficiently inferior to serve as a reminder to them and to good Christians of the Jews' spiritual decrepitude. For Christianity, the Jew was the Other, but he was the Other within, both in the sense that Jews lived in the midst of Christians and that the Jews' Book (which Christians believed the Jews had misunderstood) was part of the core narrative of Christian history.

Jews thus had a cultural significance, a radio-active charge, that was not characteristic of merchant minorities elsewhere. It was the con-fluence of their religious status as tolerated but despised outsiders, together with their eco-nomic role as merchant minority, that was so fraught. The association of the Jews with the lending of money at interest was only possible because they were beyond the community of the saved. And the association of money with a theologically stigmatized minority cast an aura of suspicion around money and moneymaking.

Had there been no Jews in Europe, the spread of capitalism would still have led to anticapital-ist movements as well as to nationalist ones. But the Jews' premodern commercial experi-ence, together with their emphasis on literacy, predisposed them to do disproportionately well in modern capitalist societies, where success increasingly depended on commercial acumen and book-learning. Anticapitalist thought would stigmatize capitalism by borrowing the con-ceptual categories of Christian anti-Semitism and the traditional condemnation of usury, of making money with money. The attempt of European states to modernize—which meant becoming literate, capitalist societies—gave rise to ethnic nationalism, which once again conceived of the Jews as outsiders.

In the face of their increasing exclusion from the ethnically defined community of the nation, Jews responded in three ways.

They migrated to countries in which nationalism was defined liberally, rather than by religious or ethnic criteria. That meant, above all, emigrating westward from Russia, where the great bulk of world Jewry was located as of 1880—westward to Austria-Hungary, to Germany, to France and to Britain, and above all, to the United States, until it closed its doors to further mass immigration in 1924. In liberal countries—even in incipiently liberal countries, like the late Habsburg Empire—Jews tended to embrace liberalism, and a program of integration into the dominant culture. While some hoped for complete assimilation and amalgamation, by and large Jews sought to acculturate to the host society without complete assimilation.[3] But the border between liberal forms of nationalism and illiberal, ethnic forms was a shifting one, and Jews repeatedly discovered that liberalizing and welcoming political cultures could turn illiberal and hostile. That is what happened in Hungary, Austria, Germany, France, and even, though in a more diluted manner, in the United States.

The second response of Jews was therefore to embrace socialist movements that promised to end invidious distinctions based on origin. Most socialists attributed the hold of anti-Semitism to capitalism itself, so that eliminating capitalism was understood as a formula for eliminating anti-Semitism. The most radical and uncompromising of these movements was Communism.

The third major response, by Jews who remained committed to some form of Jewish continuity, was Zionism. That movement drew much of its cogency from an analysis that claimed that universalist ideologies would prove a chimera. It argued that the deep-seated otherness with which the Jews were regarded in Christian and post-Christian societies would manifest itself in an increasingly nationalist era in both anticapitalist and antisocialist forms. So the early Zionist theorist, Moshe Leib Lilienblum, warned in 1883.[4] Lilienblum claimed that cosmopolitans and ethnic nationalists, capitalists and socialists, freethinkers and orthodox Christians would all find reasons to despise the Jews. For each ideological group, finding that there were Jews in the opposite camp, proceeded to identify its social or national enemy with the Jews in general.[5] In the Zionist analysis, the Jews would continue to be defined as "other"—when they were capitalists and when they were socialists, when they were assimilationist and when they were nationalist, when they were religious and when they were secular. The only solution was for the Jews to have a state of their own.

The four essays that comprise this volume explore these intertwined phenomena from a variety of perspectives. "The Long Shadow of Usury" examines the way in which the traditional linkage between Jews and money continued to be reflected in thinking by modern European intellectuals about capitalism and about the Jews. As we will see, an affirmative approach toward capitalism often went together with a measure of sympathy toward the Jews, while antipathy to commerce and antipathy to the Jews typically went hand in hand. While the first chapter explores how major non-Jewish intellectuals looked at capitalism and the Jews, the second chapter, "The Jewish Response to Capitalism," examines the other side of the coin. It takes as its launching point a lecture by the late libertarian economist Milton Friedman, who puzzled over his observation that so many Jews had been antipathetic to capitalism despite the fact that capitalism had been good for the Jews. The chapter deals with the reality of disproportionate Jewish economic success in capitalist societies, with the awareness by leading Jewish thinkers about the interconnection between capitalism and Jewry, and their interpretations and frequent affirmations of that link. Others of Jewish origin, however, reacted to capitalism and to modern anti-Semitism by embracing the most extreme form of anticapitalism, namely Communism. The fateful consequences of that embrace, which most historians have failed to appreciate, is the subject of the third chapter, "Radical Anticapitalism: The Jew as Communist." The last chapter, "The Economics of Nationalism and the Fate of the Jews in Twentieth-Century Europe," explores the relevance of the work of the late social theorist Ernest Gellner for understanding modern Jewish history. At the beginning of the twentieth century, the links between capitalism, nationalism, and the fate of the Jews had been explored by socialist Zionists, most notably Dov Ber Borochov. Gellner revived these themes at century's end, offering what seems to me the single most illuminating analysis of their relationship. He traced the link between capitalist economic development and the rise of nationalism; explained that it was precisely the Jews' traditional status as a diasporic merchant minority that led to their economic success; and showed why that placed European Jewry in particular peril in the era of ethnic nationalism.

These chapters were written to show those interested in the histories of capitalism, Communism, nationalism, Zionism, and Nazism the interconnection of these topics. Written over the past twenty years, all have been revised for publication here. The advantage of the essay form is that it allows for the exploration of broad themes without purporting to cover all relevant data. If these essays operate at a level of generalization with which historians are sometimes uncomfortable, it is because they are intended to point out patterns, to help us see the forest as well as the trees.

The subject of capitalism and the Jews can and should be understood from a variety of angles. Each chapter focuses the reader's attention on one or two of those angles. But the parts can be assembled together in a variety of ways, and I have not tried to foreclose the reader's interpretation of how they can best be fit together.

CHAPTER ONE

The Long Shadow of Usury
Capitalism and the Jews in Modern European Thought

Jews and capitalism have long been linked in the European mind. Ever since the Middle Ages, Jews were associated in the Christian West with the handling of money. It is no wonder, then, that the intellectual evaluation of an economy in which money played a central role was often intertwined with attitudes toward Jewry. Jews in Christian Europe were permitted by the church to engage in the stigmatized activity of lending money at interest precisely because they were regarded as outside the community of shared values.

For a variety of intellectuals in modern Europe, Jews served as a kind of metaphor-turned-flesh for capitalism. Some intellectuals argued that only a society in which the reality of shared community was dead would encourage the self-interested economic activities of which money-lending was the paradigm. Many intellectuals regarded Jews as the agents of the creative destruction characteristic of capitalism. They differed in their evaluation of both capitalism and of the Jews depending on how they valued the creativity unleashed by capitalism compared to its destruction of traditional forms of life and inherited privilege. Thus thinking about capitalism and thinking about the Jews often went hand in hand. Hovering above these evaluations was the specter of usury.

To our ears, the term *usury* is likely to sound archaic—a long-discarded conceptual relic of the ancient and medieval past. And so it sounded to many eighteenth-century ears as well. From John Calvin in the sixteenth century through Francis Bacon in the early seventeenth, lending at interest came to be increasingly portrayed as legitimate and necessary, if in need of restriction. John Locke inveighed against the possibility and desirability of setting a legal limit on the rate of interest in *Some Considerations of the Consequences of the Lowering of Interest, and Raising the Value of Money* of 1691. By the time we reach the age of David Hume, Adam Smith, and Jeremy Bentham in the eighteenth century, the legitimacy of lending at interest is taken entirely for granted, with attention devoted to the question of whether there were compelling social reasons for capping the interest rate, and to the broader exploration of the monetary and nonmonetary causes of interest fluctuations.[1]

But the concept of usury did not so much disappear as go underground. For usury provides one of the most long-lived paradigms for the condemnation of market activity. It combines a core propositional content with a penumbra of symbols, images, and associations that recurred not only in the eighteenth century, but in the nineteenth and twentieth as well. Indeed, its shadow extends into the twenty-first century.

The use of usury as a paradigm of stigmatization takes two forms. In the more moderate form, *usury* is employed to characterize a stigmatized form of an otherwise permitted activity. This usage of the terms grows out of medieval scholastic attempts to distinguish legitimate forms of trade from the illegitimate activity of usury. It became a term of opprobrium for those sorts of market activity that the speaker sought to condemn.

The more radical usage of the paradigm of usury was to suggest that the lending of money at interest was no different from any other form of commerce; and since the traditional condemnation of usury was morally correct, commerce itself stood condemned. This is the form that the stigma takes in its most powerful modern embodiment, Marxism. Indeed the usury paradigm provides what might be called the "deep structure" of Marx and Engels's condemnation of the market. That is to say, the condemnation of usury provides the historical origins and the conceptual underpinnings for their condemnation of capitalism. Though this may sound like an implausible claim, it was recognized by Marx and Engels themselves.

Usury was an important concept with a long shadow. It was significant because the condemnation of lending money at interest was based on the presumptive illegitimacy of all economic gain not derived from physical labor. That way of conceiving of economic activity led to a failure to recognize the role of knowledge and the evaluation of risk in economic life. It thus led to a pattern of thought quick to condemn, first, finance, and sometimes commerce more generally. And because the lending of money in medieval Europe had been linked to the Jews, that condemnation of commerce was often linked to anti-Semitism. Conversely, as we'll see, there has often been a link between philo-capitalism and philo-Semitism, with the Jews regarded as particularly valuable because of their commercial competence.

We find such a positive linkage between the

Jews and commerce in the great work of Enlightenment social science, Montesquieu's *Spirit of the Laws* of 1748. For Montesquieu, commerce had positive effects on culture and character. He famously asserted that "commerce combats destructive prejudices, and it is almost a general rule that wherever there are gentle manners (*moeurs douces*), there is commerce, and that wherever there is commerce, there are gentle manners. Therefore, one should not be surprised if our mores are less fierce than they were formerly. Commerce has spread knowledge of the mores of all nations everywhere; they are compared to each other, and from this comparison arise great advantages."[2]

Montesquieu drew a direct line between the stigmatization of usury and economic backwardness. He regarded the decline of commerce in the Middle Ages as one of the great misfortunes of European history. And he attributed that misfortune to the interpretation of usury by medieval Catholics theologians. "We owe all the misfortunes that accompanied the destruction of commerce to the speculations of the schoolmen," he wrote. For in their infatuation with the newly rediscovered philosophy of Aristotle, the Scholastics had condemned indiscriminately the taking of interest, a practice, Montesquieu thought, that was a necessary part of commerce. "Whenever one prohibits a thing that is naturally permitted or necessary, the people who engage in it are regarded as dishonest." The result was to make commerce appropriate only for those outside the faith—the Jews—and to turn them into tools of exaction by princes, who in turn oppressed the Jews. Montesquieu attributed the rise of civilization and good government in modern Europe to the Jews. For by creating bills of exchange, Jews managed to make their valuables intangible, putting their wealth beyond the oppressive hand of princes. Deprived of the ability to gain income by squeezing the Jews who in turn had squeezed the populace, princes were forced by circumstances to govern more prudently, since only good government would bring prosperity. That in turn set the stage for the rebirth of European commerce, and with it the beginning of the decline of prejudice and the rise of a more gentle, less ferocious way of life.[3]

Let us recall what usury meant and why it was condemned by the Catholic Church. Most classical writers saw no economic justification for deriving income from the merchant's role of buying and selling goods. Since the material wealth of humanity was assumed to be more or less fixed, the gain of some could only be conceived as a loss to others. Profits from trade were therefore regarded as morally suspect. But of all forms of commerce, none was so suspect and so reviled as finance, the making of money from money. Aristotle regarded the lending of money for the sake of earning interest as unnatural. "While expertise in exchange is justly blamed since it is not according to nature but involves taking from others," argued Aristotle, "usury is most reasonably hated because one's possessions derive from money itself and not from that for which it was supplied. For money was intended to be used in exchange, but not to increase at interest. . . . So of the sorts of business this is the most contrary to nature."[4] With the recovery of Aristotle's thought in the High Middle Ages, the condemnation of usury would come to occupy a central place in the economic writings of Christian theologians and canon lawyers.

This practice, which Aristotle had considered blameworthy, Christian theologians found sinful. "You may lend with interest to foreigners, but to your brother you may not lend with interest"—this verse from the twenty-third chapter of the Book of Deuteronomy had prohibited Jews from lending with interest to one another, but allowed them to lend to non-Jews. Medieval Christian and Jewish theologians strove to define the meaning of the terms *brother* and *stranger* and to provide contemporary applications. By the twelfth century, Christian theologians had concluded that the term *brother* applied to all men, and that the lending of money at interest was always sinful.[5] Usury was expressly forbidden by the Second Lateran Council in 1139.

In time, the term *usury* was applied to virtually any economic activity that was deemed immoral. The influential twelfth-century collection of canon law, the *Decretum* of Gratian, discussed the problem of sale under the general heading of usury; and the moral stigma of usury was extended to other types of contracts, especially those connected with the buying and selling of grain.[6] On a more popular level, the fable of the usurer's demise and passage to hell was a stock genre of the Middle Ages and one that appears in Dante's *Inferno*.[7]

From 1050 to 1300, new agricultural surpluses in Europe made greater commerce and urbanization possible, and that made the economic function of lending money more important. Even as theologians adapted to the rise of an urban, commercial economy by defending private property and partially legitimating trade, the opposition of the church to usury intensified.[8] Thomas Aquinas, the greatest of the Scholastics, cited both Aristotle and Roman precedents to argue that money was sterile by nature. That "money does not beget money" became central to scholastic economic doctrine.[9] From Aquinas through the eighteenth century, Catholic casuists remained vitally concerned with distinguishing profits that were usurious and hence illicit from legitimate profits.[10]

The renewed emphasis on the prohibition of usury led to a clash between religious claims and economic developments. The church struggled against usury by Christians, while money-lending was more necessary than ever to the expanding European economy. A mortal sin of theology became a mortal necessity of commercial life. "Those who engage in usury go to hell; those who fail to engage in usury fall into poverty," wrote the Italian wit, Benvenuti de Rambaldis da Imola, in his fourteenth-century commentary on Dante's *Divine Comedy*.[11]

One method by which the church resolved this dilemma, beginning in the twelfth century, was to prevent the evil of Christian usury by allowing Jews to engage in that forbidden economic activity. For Jews were not subject to the prohibitions of canon law, and were condemned in any case to perpetual damnation because of their repudiation of Christ. Pope Nicholas V, for example, preferred that "this people should perpetrate usury than that Christians should engage in it with one another."[12]

Thus began an association of moneymaking with the Jews, an association that would further taint attitudes toward commerce among Christians and that, as we well shall see, would continue to cast its shadow into the Age of Enlightenment and beyond. In Passion plays, the negotiations between Judas Iscariot and the Jewish leaders of his day were portrayed as bargaining among typical medieval Jewish moneylenders.[13] So closely was the reviled practice of usury identified with the Jews that St. Bernard of Clairvaux, the leader of the Cistercian order, in the middle of the twelfth century referred to the taking of usury as "Jewing" (*iudaizare*), and chastised Christian moneylenders as "baptized Jews."[14] In order to protect Christian moneylenders who provided them with funds, the kings of France and England created the legal fiction that these moneylenders (both lay and clerical) were to be considered Jews for legal purposes, and hence were under exclusive royal authority.[15] In central Europe, Christian moneylenders were disparaged as *Kristen-Juden*, and in the sixteenth century were chastised as wielders of the *Judenspiess*, the "Jews' skewer" of usury.[16] This symbolic identification of the forms of capitalism considered most unseemly as "Jewish" would have a long life.

As Montesquieu noted, the special role of moneylender made Jews both indispensable to the political authorities—who provided them with toleration and protection—and odious to parts of the Christian population. Jews were often brought in to meet economic needs, especially those of the monarch, for whom they were indirect tax collectors. In medieval Europe, the nobility and the clergy were exempt from royal taxation. These groups borrowed money from resident Jews and repaid their loans at substantial rates of interest. Much of the money that the Jews accumulated in this fashion made its way into the royal treasury, through royal taxes on the Jewish community or various forms of confiscation. The Jewish moneylender thus acted like a sponge, sucking up money from untaxable estates, only to be squeezed by the monarch. The interest rates charged by Jews were in keeping with the scarcity of capital in the medieval economy and the high risks incurred by Jewish moneylenders, whose loans were often canceled under public pressure, and whose assets were frequently confiscated. High by modern standards, these rates often ranged from 33 to 60 percent annually.[17]

Within western Christendom, then, the image of commerce was closely connected to that of the Jew, who was regarded as avaricious, and as an outsider and wanderer, able to engage in so reviled an activity as moneylending because he was beyond the community of shared faith.

During the Reformation, "usury" remained a stigmatized category, especially for Martin Luther. Luther's economic thought, reflected in his *Long Sermon on Usury* of 1520 and his tract *On Trade and Usury* of 1524, was hostile to commerce in general and to international trade in particular, and stricter than the canonists in its condemnation of moneylending.[18] John Calvin took issue with the scholastic view of money as sterile, and permitted the lending of money up to a fixed maximum rate of 5 percent, though he remained hostile to those who lent money by profession, and banished them from Geneva.[19] The Dutch Reformed Church followed a similar policy, sanctioning interest up to a fixed maximum, while excluding bankers from communion until the mid-seventeenth century.[20] In Protestant England, too, a similar distinction was drawn in the course of the seventeenth century between legal usury up to a fixed maximum rate of interest, and illegal usury.[21]

In Catholic countries, usury was condemned

in both canon and civil law until well into the eighteenth century, and remained an object of obloquy even later. Pope Benedict XIV reaffirmed the prohibition against lending at interest in his encyclical *Vix pervenit* of 1745, and as late as 1891 the papal encyclical *Rerum Novarum* of Leo XIII condemned "voracious usury" and linked it with greed and avarice. Usury remained an offense under French law until October 1789. To be sure, the lending of money at interest was practiced by Christians nevertheless, often furtively, sometimes with the aid of scholastic legal rationalizations that defined the transactions as nonusurious. In some places civil and even ecclesiastical courts adopted a distinction between "moderate" and "immoderate" rates of usury unsanctioned by canon law. By the mid-nineteenth century, the Vatican advised faithful Catholics who retained qualms about lending at the legal rate of interest not to worry about its effect upon their souls, but left the theoretical basis for this change of heart undecided.[22]

Yet whether the lending of money at interest was illegal in theory and subverted in practice (as in Catholic countries), or legal in theory and practice up to some limit (as in Protestant countries), the odium of the traditional connotations of usury and its connection to Jewry lingered. In the popular mind, usury was not confined to lending at interest: it was a term of opprobrium applied to any mercantile transaction regarded as unseemly or inequitable.[23]

Underlying the condemnation of merchants and moneylenders was the assumption that only those whose labor produced sweat really worked and produced. As Francis Bacon noted in his essay "Of Usury" (1612), it was widely believed that usurers were drones, and that they violated the biblical injunction that after the Fall man would live by the sweat of his brow. Most people simply could not imagine that production might be increased by the decision to invest resources in one place rather than another, with one person rather than another, in one commodity rather than another. The economic value of gathering and analyzing information simply was beyond the mental horizon of most of those who lived off the land or worked with their hands. The notion of trade—and even more, of moneylending—as unproductive was often expressed in images of parasitism. Unnatural, useless, parasitic—that was the way in which even some intellectuals thought of commerce. As we will see, many continued to do so, retaining and expanding upon the metaphors of parasitism. To the best of my knowledge, no intellectual historian has yet produced a history of the concept of usury. But the man who has come closest, Herbert Lüthy, noted of scholastic doctrine that "like alchemy or astrological magic . . . it did not die, it merely fell from the rank of science to that of a subconscious residue which nonetheless continues to act in obscure ways on the consciousness of men."[24]

In a series of steps that remain to be fully documented, the intrinsically negative connotations of usury disappear, and at least among enlightened thinkers in Protestant Europe, they vanish entirely. As we have seen, in his essay "Of Usury," Francis Bacon considers the traditional stigmatization of usury as unproductive, only to dismiss it. His concerns revolve around issues of secular public policy, recognizing the necessity of lending at interest, and asking only how widespread the practice ought to be and what levels ought to be permitted. The assumption remains that moneylending is in need of limitation and regulation, but the moral stigma has faded.[25] By the middle of the eighteenth century we have a sophisticated analysis of the causes and consequences of interest rates by David Hume, who makes only rare use of the term *usury*, and does so with no invidious connotations whatsoever.[26] In his *Defence of Usury* of 1787, Jeremy Bentham took issue with

Adam Smith's suggestion that interest rates be capped to prevent the flow of funds to prodigals and projectors, arguing persuasively that entrepreneurs with really new ideas were typically dismissed as "projectors" and that Smith's suggestion would dry up funds for entrepreneurial innovation.[27] Benjamin Franklin turned the Aristotelian tenet of the unfruitfulness of money on its head. In his essay "Advice to a Young Tradesman, Written by an Old One" (1748), Franklin writes, "Remember, that Money is of a prolific generating Nature. Money can beget Money, and its Offspring can beget more, and so on."

Voltaire provides a notable exception. The most renowned intellectual of the Enlightenment, Voltaire was a contemporary of Montesquieu, Hume, and Franklin. That makes his use of the term *usury* all the more striking. For Voltaire used *usury* not as a category of economic analysis, but as an epithet of stigmatization associated with Jews, and linked to dishonesty and avarice.

Time and again Voltaire was accused by those who knew him of just those negative attributes that the Christian tradition had associated with mercantile activity: dishonesty and avarice. In England, where Voltaire spent the years from 1726 to 1728, he was accused of shady business practices, and his banker there concluded that "Voltaire is very avaricious and dishonest." Friedrich the Great and Gotthold Ephraim Lessing, who knew Voltaire when he took up residence at Friedrich's estate in Potsdam, termed his financial practices those of a scoundrel. Voltaire's lover, Mme. Denis, wrote to him that he was "pierced by avarice." "Your heart makes you the lowest of men," she wrote, "but I will hide the vices of your heart as best I can."[28] Voltaire reacted by denouncing the Jews as the embodiment of the vices of which he was so frequently accused—a classic case of projection.

In his historical writings and in historical references scattered throughout his works, Voltaire not only characterized contemporary Jews as avaricious usurers, but attributed these characteristics to Jews throughout the ages, beginning with the biblical Hebrews. According to Voltaire, Abraham was so avaricious that he prostituted his wife for money; David slew Goliath not to protect his people, but for economic gain; Herod was unable to complete the rebuilding of the temple in Jerusalem because the Jews, though they loved their sanctuary, loved their money more.[29] Jewish avarice and usury thus appeared as ongoing, racial characteristics. Voltaire's *Philosophical Dictionary* is replete with references to the inherently usurious nature of the Jews. In the article titled "The Heaven of the Ancients," he wrote of the biblical Hebrews that "their only science was the trade of jobbery and usury."[30] In addition to picturing Jews as avaricious usurers, Voltaire frequently portrayed them as dishonest in their economic dealings.

Of course Voltaire's antipathy to Jews and Judaism had other sources as well. He hated Judaism as the progenitor of Christianity; and in order to evade censorship he sometimes criticized Christianity by allusion through his direct attacks on Judaism. As the intellectual historian John Pocock has observed, "Voltaire's hatred of the Jews is not racial, or even the hatred of an Other, so much as it is hatred of that within his own civilization which he most detested; almost a hatred of self."[31] Though Voltaire was vehement in his antipathy to Christianity, one of the few elements of his Christian heritage that he managed to preserve was the link between the stigmatization of moneylending and of the Jews. Perhaps this reflected a psychological need to deflect the traditional accusations against commerce hurled—with good cause—against Voltaire himself, by projecting them upon the Jews. In any event, it revived a much older pattern, by which those aspects of economic activity deemed most threatening were attributed to the Jews.

The Jew as avaricious usurer and economic parasite remained a recurring theme in the Age of Enlightenment.[32] But it was in the nineteenth century that the complex of ideas associated with usury would find more influential modern exponents. Nowhere is the paradigm of usury more important than in the work of Karl Marx and Friedrich Engels.

In an early essay of 1844, "Outlines of a Critique of Political Economy," Engels laid out in embryonic form many of the ideas that he and Marx were to spend the rest of their lives developing.[33] The essence of Engels's critique of political economy as it had developed in the work of Adam Smith and his disciples was that it obscured the basic truth that capitalism was built on avarice and on selfishness. If the key maneuver of Enlightenment thinkers such as Smith was to call attention to the potential social benefits of what had been previously stigmatized as "greed" and "pride," the first countermaneuver of socialist critics like Engels was to restigmatize self-interest as greed.[34] For Engels, trade stood condemned, in the first instance, for the *impurity of motivation* that lay behind it. Morality, by definition, could not be based on self-interest.

If Engels's first step was to go back to pre-Enlightenment understandings of self-interest, his second was to reach back further, to medieval condemnations of the interest on loans. Profits from trade, he reasoned, were little different from "interest" and could only be distinguished from it by overly subtle logic-chopping. And interest was immoral: "The immorality of lending at interest, of receiving without working . . . has long ago been recognized for what it is by unprejudiced popular consciousness, which in such matters is usually right."[35]

That capitalists received without working would become the controlling premise of the theoretical framework developed by Engels's great collaborator. Karl Marx's background and personality help account for fundamental elements of his social theory. Marx was the son of a highly secularized Jewish father, Heinrich Marx, who had converted to Lutheranism in order to be able to practice law in Prussia. Heinrich's wife converted shortly thereafter, and the couple had their children converted, including Karl, their eldest son. Karl Marx's origin was as a member of a minority, stigmatized for its religion, regarded as a separate nationality, and disdained for its economic role. His vision of the Communist future posited a society in which religious and national differences would be obliterated, and moneymaking abolished.

A milestone in the development of Marx's critique of capitalism is his essay "On the Question of the Jews" (*Zur Judenfrage*), published in 1844 alongside Engels's critique of political economy. In this contribution to a long-simmering controversy among German liberal and radical writers, Marx combined his moral critique of capitalism with traditional anti-Jewish images, not in order to bolster anti-Semitism, but to blacken the moral standing of capitalist society.

The question of the status of the Jews was much debated among German political writers in the first half of the nineteenth century—by one estimate, 2,500 works were published on the issue between 1815 and 1850, by writers Jewish and non-Jewish.[36] In 1843, the debate on what to do about the Jews was ignited within Marx's own circle with the publication of two works by Bruno Bauer, a radical Hegelian colleague with whom Marx had planned to publish the "Archives of Atheism."

Bauer combined a philosophical attack on granting Jews civil and political equality with a portrait of Jewry etched in acid. (Later on he would abandon his philosophical radicalism, while maintaining his antipathy to the Jews.) He characterized Judaism as a religion of egoism, a recurrent theme among German philosophical radicals. The Jews were uninterested in culture, science, and philosophy, Bauer claimed. He attacked them above all for their particularism, evidence of which he found in the fact that they remained outside the guilds and instead engaged in usury.[37] It was this link between particularism, egoism, and usury on which Marx would focus. Marx's response was to insist that, despite his purported radicalism, Bauer's analysis was not nearly radical enough.

Were the Jews egoistic, as Bauer had charged? Certainly, Marx answered. But in bourgeois society, *everyone* was egoistic. Were the Jews particularistic? Of course, but in bourgeois, capitalist society, there *was* no interest but the particular interest. Was Bauer correct in characterizing the Jew as a "constrained being"? Yes, Marx replied, because in bourgeois society, all were constrained. Did the Jews cut themselves off from others? Yes, because that is what "rights" meant in a liberal, market society: the right to be particular, to be egoistic, to be constrained and encapsulated. All of these qualities followed from the highest of liberal rights: the right to private property.

In bringing his argument to its crescendo, Marx played on the multiple meanings of the German word *Judentum*. It could mean Judaism (the religion), the Jews (as a group), or, like its English equivalent "jewing," a synonym for bargaining, fraught with negative connotations. Marx also uses a second term with multiple connotations, *Schacher*. The word was a colloquialism, which is often translated as "haggling," as retail trading involving bargaining. But that is to miss its resonance for Marx's contemporaries. Like the English term *huckstering*, it was used figuratively to mean "a person ready to make his profit of anything in a mean and petty way." It also was a popular term for "usury." The shared element in these meanings came from the fact that *Schacher* was virtually always associated with Jews. Indeed the word itself is derived from the root of the Hebrew term for trade, *sachar*. Excluded from many areas of the German economy by law and custom, Jews often eked out a living by peddling, trading in whatever items they could buy and sell, including secondhand goods, and by lending money. Especially in rural areas little served by merchants and banks, Jews played all of these roles. In a society of lords and peasants, they were among the few who regularly engaged in calculating the relative value of items, and the chances of making a profit by buying and selling. *Schacher*, therefore, connoted the stigmatized economic activities that were typically associated with Jews. Marx made use of the multiple connotations of *Schacher* to lay out his critique of market society:

> Let us seek the secret of the Jew not in his religion, rather let us seek for the secret of religion in the real Jew.
>
> What is the worldly basis of Jewdom? *Practical* need, *self-interest*.
>
> What is the worldly cult of the Jew? *Bargaining* [*Schacher*]. What is his worldly god? *Money*.
>
> Well, then! The self-emancipation of our age would be emancipation from *bargaining* and from *money*, that is from practical, real Jewdom....
>
> The Jew has emancipated himself in a Jewish way not only by acquiring financial power, but also because through him and without him, *money* has become a world power and the practical Jewish spirit has become the practical spirit of the Christian peoples. The Jews

have emancipated themselves insofar as the Christians have become Jews.[38]

Marx embraces all of the traditional negative characterizations of the Jew repeated by Bauer, and for good measure adds a few of his own. But he does so in order to stigmatize market activity as such. For Marx's strategy is to endorse every negative characterization of market activity that Christians associated with Jews, but to insist that those qualities have now come to characterize society as a whole, very much including Christians. The Christian tradition of stigmatizing Jews and the economic activities in which they engaged by virtue of their marginality now becomes a stick with which to beat bourgeois society as a whole.

Like Voltaire a century earlier, Marx condemns the Jews for their stubborn particularism. For Marx, the market represents the universalization of particular interests. If, in a capitalist society, Christians too are egoistic and particularistic, then the fact that Christianity is more universalistic than Judaism ceases to matter. Not only religious difference is to be overcome: all self-interest, individual and group, is to be eliminated.

In the second half of his essay, Marx takes on

Bauer's claim that the Jews are devoid of interest in higher culture, in philosophy, in man as an end in himself. True enough, Marx says. But in contemporary bourgeois society, *everyone* takes on the characteristics of the moneyman, who is typically uninterested in anything but getting richer. Though the Jews are narrow and confined, so is all of life in bourgeois society.

At the end of his essay, Marx takes Bauer's claim that Christianity is a more universal religion than Judaism and gives it an ironic twist. It is under the universalist auspices of Christianity that a truly universalist process is occurring, the spread of the market (bourgeois society). But it is universal in that all collective human ties are torn apart by egoism, by self-interested need, and dissolved into a world of atomistic individuals practicing relations of enmity.

The true God of the Jews is money, Marx assures his readers, and like the jealous God of the Bible, who would tolerate no lesser gods before him, money tolerates no other relations: it transforms all natural objects and human relationships into commodities that can be exchanged. Radical Hegelians claimed that God ought to be understood as the alienated essence of man, in which human characteristics of love and power are projected onto an illusory master to whom men subordinated themselves. So too, Marx suggests, with money, which "is the alienated essence of man's labor and his being," an alien being that dominates him, and that he reveres. Hence Marx's ironic conclusion, "The *social* emancipation of the Jew is the *emancipation of society from Jewdom.*"

"On the Question of the Jews" is Janus-faced. Read carefully, Marx's argument is clear enough: all of the negative moral evaluations that traditional Christian and modern post-Christians like Voltaire and Bauer applied to Jews should in fact be applied to capitalist society. But because Marx himself reiterated so many negative characterizations of the Jews and their economic role, with a twist of the argument one could suggest that the task was to rescue capitalism from its "Jewish" aspects, and from the Jews themselves. That would be the theme, with variations, of subsequent anti-Jewish authors from Richard Wagner down to the Nazi ideologist Gottfried Feder.

It would be only a slight exaggeration to say that the rest of Marx's career was an attempt to prove these claims, first set out in 1844, when he was twenty-six years old. For "On the Question of the Jews" contains, in embryo, most of the subsequent themes of Marx's critique of capitalism: the labor theory of value, the power of money (i.e., capital), the elimination of cultural particularity through the spread of the market, the fetishization of commodities.

If Marx had one big idea, it was that capitalism was the rule of money—itself the expression of greed. The rule of capital was fundamentally immoral because it deprived the vast majority in a capitalist society of their humanity, requiring labor that enriched a few capitalists while impoverishing the workers physically and spiritually. Men were thus at the mercy of inimical forces that they felt they could not control. Yet in "bourgeois ideology" these forces were treated as natural and inexorable. This set of ideas was not the *conclusion* of his years of inquiry into the capitalist economy—it was the never-abandoned *premise* of that inquiry. The world he imagined would be free of discrimination against Jews because Judaism, together with other religious and collective identities, would evaporate. It would also be a world without "Jewdom" since the egoism and particularism ascribed to the Jews and central to capitalism would be eliminated. It would be a world of great wealth, but without specie. For money—capital—was evil, and the gaining of money from money unjust.

If Marx's vision was forward-looking, its premises were curiously archaic. For him, self-interest is the enemy of social cohesion and of morality. In that sense, Marx's thought is a reversion to a time before Hegel, Adam Smith, or Montesquieu. Marx himself came to recognize how much he shared with the pre-Enlightenment critique of commerce. In his *Theories of Surplus Value* (written 1861–63), he quotes from Bernard de Mandeville's contention in *The Fable of the Bees* (1706) that all of trade and commerce is based on evil (*das Böse*). "Mandeville," Marx comments, "was of course infinitely more intrepid and honest than the philistine apologists of bourgeois society."[39] Quoting Luther's tirades against moneylenders, Marx noted that the founder of Protestantism "has really caught the character of old-fashioned usury, and that of capital as a whole."[40]

Capital expanded upon Marx's earlier ideas, without altering them fundamentally. The book's argument rests on the labor theory of value. And the labor theory of value asserts that capital is fundamentally unproductive. Thus the chapter of *Capital* entitled "The General Formula of Capital" has one main point: that capital is money that makes money, even if in capitalist society it does so through the intermediary stage of the merchant who buys and sells commodities or the industrialist who buys and sells labor. Or in Marx's resonant image,

"The capitalist knows that all commodities—however shabby they may look or bad they may smell—are in faith and in fact money, internally circumcised Jews, and in addition magical means by which to make more money out of money." Here capital is not only identified with the Jews, but is endowed with the "Jewish stench" attributed to Jews in Christian Europe since medieval times.[41] All the traditional prejudices against usury were now reformulated as a critique of the market in the age of industry. The book is replete with images of parasitism, vampirism, and even cannibalism.

"Capital is dead labor which, vampire-like, lives only by sucking living labor, and lives the more, the more labor it sucks. The time during which the worker works is the time during which the capitalist consumes the labor-power he has bought from him."[42] Marx sustains the metaphors of vampirism, werewolfism,[43] and cannibalism through much of his discussion of the condition of the worker under capitalism. By virtue of the "voracious hunger for surplus labor,"[44] the capitalist is constantly seeking to increase the number of hours that the worker must toil, and thus "the means of production consume the worker as the ferment necessary to their own life-process."[45] When Lenin later referred to the necessity of eliminating capitalists because they were "bloodsuckers," he was merely heightening Marx's own metaphor. For Marx, as for Luther, money—now rechristened "capital"—is fundamentally unproductive. Those who wield it do so at the expense of others. Indeed the Marxist theory of "exploitation" acquires much of its resonance from its continuity with the notion that capitalists, like usurers, grow rich by not working, by unjustly living off the work of others.

Marx was by no means the first to connect the critique of capitalism with the traditional stigmatization of usury—nor was he the last. A year after Marx published his essay "On the Jewish Question," in 1844, Alphonse Toussenel published his *Les Juifs, rois de l'époque* (1845), in which he denounced the new feudalism of finance, at the center of which stood Jewish bankers and usurers, along with their British and Protestant allies. His argument was reiterated in an even more radical form by Edouard Drumont in *La France juive*, published in 1886.[46] For much of the later nineteenth century, the attack on finance took the form of an attack on the Jews, and especially on the Rothschilds, the personifications of Jewish finance.[47]

Nowhere was the intellectual exploration of the origins, nature, and moral significance of capitalism pursued with greater intensity than in Germany at the turn of the twentieth century. At its highest levels, it took the form of a three-way debate between Georg Simmel (1858–1918), Max Weber (1864–1920), and Werner Sombart (1863–1941). The role of Jews and of finance were central to the debate, either explicitly or implicitly.

Much of the stimulus for the debate came from Simmel's remarkable work *The Philosophy of Money*, published in 1900.

A religious outsider by familial origin but a religious insider by upbringing (his ancestors were Jewish, but his parents had converted to Lutheranism), a member of the upper middle class living at the cultural and commercial crossroads of German life, fluent in French and cosmopolitan in orientation, Simmel was keenly sensitive to the burgeoning possibilities of modern life.[48]

Simmel explored the psychological effects of living in an economy in which more and more areas of life could be measured in money. Such an economy created a mind-set that was more abstract, because the means of exchange were themselves becoming ever more abstract. Exchange had begun as barter, the very tangible giving of one thing for another. Later, in an early stage of a money economy, the means of exchange—gold, silver, or other precious metal—was itself of intrinsic value. In an advanced economy, money is comprised of pieces of metal or paper, the value of which is ultimately guaranteed only by the power of the central state: a mark is worth a mark, or a dollar a dollar, because the issuing government says so and has the ability to protect the economy against shocks that would destroy it. With the development of credit, money becomes more abstract still, little more than a bookkeeping notation.[49] Through constant exposure to an abstract means of exchange, individuals under capitalism are habituated to thinking about the world in a more abstract manner.

They also become more calculating and more used to weighing factors in making decisions. Where one is dependent on the market for almost everything from food to entertainment to medicine, decisions about how to live become decisions about what to buy; choices about how to live better become choices of how much of one thing to trade off for another. Because each of these decisions requires calculations of more or less—if I pay more for item X, I'll have less left over for item Y—people in a money economy become acclimated to thinking in numerical terms. This numerical, calculating style of thought spills over into more and more personal decisions. Life becomes more cool and calculated, less impulsive and emotional.[50]

Life in a modern, money economy, Simmel stressed, is characterized by ever greater distances between means and ends. Determining how to attain our ends is a matter of intellect: of calculation, weighing, comparing the various possible means to reach our goals most efficiently. Thus intellect, concerned with the weighing of means, comes to play an ever greater role.

While Simmel could at times echo the complaints of cultural pessimists and of cultural critics of capitalism, at his most creative he upended their assumptions. Unlike Marx and Engels, who decried the competitive process so central to capitalism as intrinsically evil, Simmel pointed out the integrative effects of competition. For competition was not a relationship between those who competed only, it was a struggle for the affection—or money—of a third party. To compete successfully, Simmel noted, the competitor must devote himself to discovering the desires of that third party. As a result, competition often "achieves what usually only love can do: the divination of the innermost wishes of the other, even before he himself becomes aware of them. Antagonistic tension with his competitor sharpens the businessman's sensitivity to the tendencies of the public, even to the point of clairvoyance, regarding future changes in the public's tastes, fashions, interests." And the competition for customers and consumers had a highly democratic aspect as well. "Modern competition," Simmel observed, "is often described as the fight of all against all, but at the same time it is the fight of all *for* all." Thus, he concluded, competition forms "a web of a thousand social threads: through concentrating the consciousness on the will and feeling and thinking of fellowmen, through the adaptation of producers to consumers, through the discovery of ever more refined possibilities of gaining their favor and patronage."[51]

In *The Philosophy of Money* and in his other works, Simmel explained that the development of the market economy made for new possibilities of individuality. Simmel suggested that the limited-liability corporation was a model for many characteristic forms of association under advanced capitalism, in which individuals cooperate with a limited portion of their lives for common but limited purposes. Compared to the precapitalist past, in which individuals lived most of their lives in a single, circumscribed community, modern life was based upon looser, more temporary associations, founded to pursue specific economic, cultural, or political interests, and demanding of the individual only a small part of himself, sometimes only a monetary contribution in the form of dues. As a result, the modern individual can belong to a greater range of groups, but groups that are looser and less encompassing. Thus Simmel concluded that "money establishes incomparably more connections among people than ever existed in the days of the feudal associations so beloved by romantics."[52] In contrast to earlier forms of association, modern groups allow for participation without absorption. They make it possible for the individual to develop a variety of interests and to become involved in a wider range of activities than would otherwise be possible, yet to do so without surrendering the totality of his time, income, or identity to any particular association, from the family to the state.[53] For Simmel, the eclipse of "community" was not a source of nostalgic lament: it presented new possibilities, along with potential pitfalls. He highlighted the development of a new form of individuality promoted by the market economy, an individuality based on choice from among the many cultural spheres and social circles created by the capitalist market.

On the surface, *The Philosophy of Money* would seem to have little to say about the questions that would exercise Max Weber and Werner Sombart, namely the origins of capitalism and accounting for the role of the Jews in it. But, writing before *The Protestant Ethic* or *The Jews and Modern Capitalism*, Simmel offered his own anticipatory answers to these issues.

While *The Philosophy of Money* draws on a remarkable range of historical data, it provides no genetic account of the "origin" of modern capitalism. That seems to be because Simmel believes there is no historical "break" that marks the beginning of modern capitalism. Rather, modern capitalism is an intensification of processes of exchange that have been going on for a very long time. The greater intensity of monetary exchange itself brings about changes in mentality. Thus there is no need for the sort of cultural explanation offered by Weber and Sombart, who assumed that modern capitalism represented a qualitative break from previous patterns of economic life, and that this break had to be accounted for in terms of the psychological effects of religious dispositions—of Calvinist Protestantism for Weber, and of Judaism for Sombart. Simmel accounted for the Jews' disproportionate participation in early modern capitalism in terms of their social and political position in medieval Europe (one that to be sure was linked to Christian theological premises about the Jew as outside the community of the saved). Unlike Weber, Simmel does not discount the significance of exchange in explaining the genesis and nature of capitalism. And unlike Sombart, Simmel does not think that an explanation based on the content of Judaism or the racial characteristics of the Jews is necessary to account for their success. On the contrary, Simmel's emphasis is on the way the Jews' mentality can best be explained by their economic condition.[54]

"The importance of money as a means, independent of all specific ends, results in the fact that money becomes the center of interest and the proper domain of individuals and classes who, because of their social position, are excluded from many kinds of personal and specific goals," Simmel writes. He goes on to cite Armenians in Turkey, Parsees in India, Huguenots in France, and Quakers in England as examples of this phenomenon, before noting, "There is no need to emphasize that the Jews are the best example of the correlation between the central role of money interests and social deprivation." Simmel emphasizes the fact that such cultural outsiders are attracted to financial and exchange functions because money provides them with opportunities otherwise closed to them, since they are excluded from the personal channels open to the dominant in-group. The existence of diaspora networks serves to encourage employment in trade and finance, rather than in primary production. Thus social exclusion and diasporic circumstances are the key factors in accounting for why Jews have tended to be drawn to the money aspects of the economy.

But for Simmel, this does not make them marginal to the process of capitalist development (as Weber would suggest) or central to the genesis of capitalism, as Sombart would argue. Rather it makes the Jews disproportionately successful at a phenomenon that is central to the modern world, and, on the whole, to be welcomed.

Max Weber, who stemmed from a family of Calvinist entrepreneurs who sometimes turned to politics, is best known today for his studyof the origins of modern capitalism, *The Protestant Ethic and the Spirit of Capitalism*, first published in 1904–5.[55] But the exploration and explanation of capitalism was central to much of his work, including his writings of the 1890s on contemporary stock and commodity exchanges.[56]

Weber was a liberal and a nationalist. The liberal cast of Weber's nationalism was evident in the way in which he treated the economic role of the Jews. They were conspicuously absent from his contemporary analysis. While liberal nationalism regarded all those within the borders of the nation as equal citizens, illiberal, integral nationalists insisted that only those who shared a common past—religious, cultural, and biological—were truly part of the nation. In France, Germany, and much of eastern Europe, integral nationalism portrayed the peasant and the artisan as the heart of the nation and its culture.[57] The *bêtes noires* of integral nationalism were those who engaged in commerce, and above all the quintessence of commerce, the stock and commodity exchanges. Jews, who had long been involved in trade, were overrepresented among those on the exchanges, and so it was but a small leap for contemporary anti-Semites to identify the exchanges with the Jews. Weber wrote an extensive defense of the stock and commodity exchanges at a time when they were under attack, and without mentioning the salience of the Jews in their operation.[58]

Throughout his career, Weber insisted that capitalism was the most efficient economic system possible under modern conditions. While he was ambivalent about its cultural effects, he devoted himself to dispelling the most frequent accusations against it, as in his defense of the stock and commodity exchanges in the 1890s. In the new preface for *The Protestant Ethic and the Spirit of Capitalism* written toward the end of his life, Weber took issue with those who identified capitalism with unscrupulous greed. The impulse of acquisition, he wrote, was not in itself a defining characteristic of capitalism. That desire exists at all times. "It should be taught in the kindergarten of cultural history that this naive idea of capitalism must be given up once and for all. *Unlimited greed for gain is not in the least identical with capitalism, and is still less its spirit,*" Weber asserted,[59] for in fact, "the universal reign of absolute unscrupulousness in the pursuit of selfish interests by the making of money has been a specific characteristic of precisely those countries whose bourgeois-capitalistic development . . . has remained backward." He dubbed the notion that modern capitalism is characterized by greater *greed* than other forms of life "the illusions of modern romanticists."[60]

In *The Protestant Ethic*, as in his later writings on capitalism, Weber emphasized its rationality but especially the "rational, industrial organization, attuned to a regular market, and not to political or irrational speculative opportunities for profit" as the distinguishing element of modern capitalism. The whole realm of finance and investment—the rational calculation of possibilities for the use of capital, in which Jews had excelled—was slighted in Weber's definition.

It was highlighted, by contrast, in the work of Weber's colleague, Werner Sombart. Among the most renowned social scientists of his day, Sombart in his work spanned the disciplines of history, economics, and sociology. The term *capitalism* came into academic social science by way of his book *Modern Capitalism* (*Der moderne Kapitalismus*), published in 1902. Written in an accessible and pointed style, Sombart's books reached far beyond the academy. According to him, capitalism meant the decline of culture worthy of the name, and those most responsible for that decline were the Jews. His work linked romantic anticapitalist communitarianism with anti-Semitism.

The first of Sombart's works to combine economic history with romantic anticapitalism was *Die deutsche Volkswirtschaft im neunzehnten Jahrhundert* (*The German Economy in the Nineteenth Century*), published in 1903. He portrayed the precapitalist economy of the artisan and peasant as "natural" and the modern capitalist economy as "artificial." Sombart shared the romantic prejudice that identified the archaic with the authentic. He treated the forms of life characteristic of the less modernized groups in the population as primordial, though they were in fact the product of earlier historical development. For Sombart, capitalism's dissolution of the traditional way of life of the *Volk* was leading to the "graveyard of culture." While capitalism marked a quantitative gain— he recognized that it was more productive and created a higher material standard of living—it meant a loss in the quality of life, robbing men of inner peace, of their relationship to nature, and of the faith of their fathers. It led to overvaluing the things of this world. (Like many romantic conservatives, Sombart was not religious, but he thought it a pity that others were not.) Capitalism, according to Sombart, destroyed the soul and led to the standardization or "massification" of cultural life. Though he lived his entire life in major cities, Sombart saw nothing positive in the process of urbanization: he stigmatized city life as an artificial, inauthentic form of existence, producing what he dismissively dubbed "asphalt culture."

In the same book, Sombart began to draw attention to what was to become a leitmotif of his writing and lecturing for the next decade— the link between capitalism and the Jews. The Jewish mind, he insisted, was characterized by egoism, self-interest, and abstraction: precisely the qualities most suited for capitalism. His key witness for the elective affinity between capitalism and Jewish character was none other than Karl Marx, whose work "On the Question of the Jews" Sombart quoted with approval: "What is the worldly basis of Jewdom? *Practical need, self-interest*. What is the worldly cult of the Jew? *Bargaining*. What is his worldly god? *Money*." In 1911, six years after Max Weber published his essays on the Protestant ethic, Sombart published his response, *The Jews and Economic Life* (*Die Juden und das Wirtschaftsleben*), in which he sought to show that it was the Jews who had been crucial to the rise of modern capitalism, and that they had played so large a role in it because they were spiritually and culturally inclined to the rationalistic and calculative mentality so characteristic of capitalism. According to Sombart, it was the Jewish religion itself that predisposed Jews toward capitalism, for it was the religion of a rootless, nomadic "desert people," given to abstraction, a contractual conception of their relationship with God, and the numerical calculation of sin. Jews were accustomed to living their lives teleologically, orienting their lives to a distant goal, Sombart speculated. They were therefore used to thinking of things as means to an end. Money, he noted, was a pure means. Therefore, Sombart concluded, Jews were particularly attentive to money, as the means par excellence. Jews, according to Sombart, were inclined less to the creative, entrepreneurial elements of capitalism than to the calculative search for advantage characteristic of finance and trade. And this calculating, means-weighing, abstract numerical mind fitted the Jew to be "the perfect stock-exchange speculator." Sombart portrayed the triumph of capitalism as the replacement of a concrete, particularist, Christian community (*Gemeinschaft*) by an abstract, universalistic, judaized society.

As one looks back at the triangular debate between Simmel, Weber, and Sombart, Simmel's contributions seem most prescient. He emphasized the primacy of exchange (trade and finance) in explaining capitalism; he was implicitly skeptical of the existence of a clearly-definable break between the precapitalist and capitalist eras, a break claimed by both Sombart and Weber; he accounted for Jewish involvement in exchange by virtue of historical circumstances rather than by reference to the intrinsic content of Judaism or inherent racial propensities; and he neither downplayed nor overstated the role of the Jews in capitalist development. Last but not least, he presented a conception of man under advanced capitalism that was far richer and more open than the caricatures of the purposeless accumulator or the spiritless professional (*Berufsmenschentum*) that haunt the pages of Weber's *Protestant Ethic*, or the soulless calculator of Sombart's *The Jews and Modern Capitalism*.

Sombart's identification of the Jews with the elements of capitalism that he most deplored provided a scholarly patina for what was already one of the most frequent motifs of anti-Semites in Germany, as in Britain and France, who held the Jews responsible for everything they despised about capitalism and the modern world.[61] Leading German anti-Semitic authors, in turn, pillaged Sombart's work for evidence to buttress their cause. Theodor Fritsch, the author of *The Anti-Semitic Catechism*, who was later honored by the Nazis as their *Altmeister*, published *The Jews in Commerce and the Secret of Their Success* (*Die Juden im Handel und das Geheimnis ihrer Erfolgen*) in 1913, a book that paraphrased Sombart's arguments for hundreds of pages on end, while criticizing him for being insufficiently hostile to the Jews.[62] We find the same stigmatization of financial activity in the musings of the Nazi economic theorist Gottfried Feder, author of, among other works, *A*

Manifesto on Breaking Monetary Interest Slavery (*Das Manifest zur Brechung der Zinsknechtschaft des Geldes*). The official platform of the Nazi party, which Feder helped write, called for "the breaking of interest slavery," echoing the condemnation of usury. In a later work, *The Struggle Against High Finance* (*Kampf gegen Hochfinanz*), published in 1933, Feder distinguished between Aryan and Jewish forms of capitalism, the former industrial and creative, the latter financial and parasitic.[63] Here was the quintessence of attempts to stigmatize disfavored forms of capitalist activity as Jewish.

Even so liberal a figure as the British economist John Maynard Keynes associated the elements of capitalism that he liked least with the Jews. That is not to suggest that the content of Keynes's economics was anti-Jewish, only that his more speculative writings are redolent of the prejudicial association of Judaism with the features of capitalism from which he sought to distance himself, and eventually, his society.

Keynes associated the Jews with deferred gratification at the expense of the enjoyment of life. While Keynes's head was in the mathematics and economics of Cambridge, his heart was in the London neighborhood of Bloomsbury, where his cultural sensibilities were shaped by his participation in its famed and flamboyant circle of artists, musicians, and writers. From the heights of Bloomsbury he looked down at the City of London, the center of finance. From early on, he portrayed the price of economic progress as the cultural deformation of those he invidiously dubbed the "rentier bourgeoisie," who had sacrificed the "arts of enjoyment" to "compound interest."[64]

These sentiments were on display in a startling and much-reprinted lecture published in 1930 as "Economic Prospects for Our Grandchildren." Keynes noted the remarkable past performance of capitalism as an engine of economic growth, and predicted that if war and internal instability could be avoided, its future performance could be as dramatic. Indeed, Keynes speculated that mankind was on its way to solving its "economic problem." Within a few generations, a society was within sight in which the problem would be how to spend one's leisure time when there was so little necessary labor to be done.

The problem for Keynes was deferred gratification, what he called "purposiveness," the focus on means over ends, which boiled down to being "more concerned with the remote future results of our actions than with their own quality or their immediate effects on our own environment." He disparaged this elevation of the future over the present as an attempt "to secure a spurious and delusive immortality." In a rhetorical flourish worthy of Marx or Sombart, Keynes identified this deferred gratification with the quest for immortality, with usury, and with the Jews. "Perhaps it is not an accident that the race which did most to bring the promise of immortality into the heart and essence of our religions has also done the most for the principle of compound interest and particularly loves this most purposive of human institutions," he declared. In the more affluent future, Keynes declared:

> I see us free . . . to return to some of the most sure and certain principles of religion and traditional virtue—that avarice is a vice, that the exaction of usury is a misdemeanour, and the love of money is detestable, that those walk most truly in the paths of virtue and sane wisdom who take least thought for tomorrow. We shall once more value ends above means and prefer the good to the useful. We shall honour those who can teach us how to pluck the hour and the day virtuously and well, the delightful people who are capable of taking direct enjoyment in things, the lilies of the field who toil not, neither do they spin.

Such were the prospects two generations hence, Keynes thought. Individualism would flourish, shorn of its unlovely, Jewish features.[65] For the moment, however, the fundamental moral hypocrisy behind capitalist society would have to continue: "We must go on pretending that fair is foul and foul is fair; for foul is useful and fair is not. Avarice and usury and precaution must be our goods for a little longer still. For only they can lead us out of the tunnel of economic necessity into the daylight." In the meantime, it was people like his Bloomsbury companions who were the seeds of a more cultivated future. Even Keynes, then, labored under the long shadow of usury, though there was no discernable link between Keynes's formal economic theory and his anti-Jewish prejudices.

A linkage between capitalism and the Jews also appears in the work of Keynes's sometime antagonist, Friedrich A. Hayek. But for Hayek, as for Montesquieu and Simmel before him, the link between Jews and capitalism is a positive one.

Born in Vienna in 1899, when it was still the capital of the Austro-Hungarian empire, Hayek came of age intellectually in the highly antiliberal culture of Vienna of the 1920s and in the shadow of Communism and fascism. In inter-war Vienna, the rhetoric of anticapitalism and anti-Semitism were often closely intertwined. The three major political groupings vied with one another to link capitalism and the Jews, always invidiously. Even the Social Democrats, who officially condemned anti-Semitism and who had dubbed it "the socialism of fools," resorted to anti-Semitic imagery in the interests of anticapitalism.

Hayek's liberalism was not a typical product of Vienna: like much of what has come to be considered "Viennese culture" it was produced *against* its Viennese environment.[66] Hayek was not Jewish and wrote relatively little about the Jews. But his liberalism was influenced by his close contacts with Jews in Vienna, at a time when many others of his class—including members of his own family and his leading academic teacher—favored attempts to exclude those of Jewish origin from economic, cultural, and political life. For Hayek, Jews were prototypical of the sort of person whose talents led to economic progress, but whose success was resented by the mass of the population.

For Hayek, in a capitalist society everybody becomes in some measure an entrepreneur, on the lookout for the more effective use of resources. But not every group would be equal in its resourcefulness. A central theme of Hayek's liberalism was the role of the innovative few in bringing about historical advance. But the progress created by the resourceful few—while it brought long-term benefits to society at large—came at the expense of some established social groups. Hayek regarded fascism and Nazism as the desperate attempt by social losers in the process of capitalist development to regain the rewards denied them in the marketplace through force and ideological special pleading. In *The Road to Serfdom* of 1944, he portrayed fascism and Nazism as a socialism of the middle classes. What socialism, Fascism, and National Socialism shared, according to Hayek, was the notion that the state "should assign to each person his proper place in society." Fascism and Nazism were so successful "because they offered a theory, or *Weltanschauung*, which seemed to justify the privileges they promised to their supporters."

For Hayek, there was a close link between anticapitalism and anti-Semitism, not least because the Jews embodied precisely those characteristics that were essential to capitalist progress. In his *Road to Serfdom* he noted that

> in Germany and Austria, the Jew had come to be regarded as the representative of capitalism

because a traditional dislike of large classes of the population for commercial pursuits had left these more readily accessible to a group that was practically excluded from the more highly esteemed occupations. It is the old story of the alien race's being admitted only to the less respected trades and then being hated still more for practicing them. The fact that German anti-Semitism and anti-capitalism spring from the same root is of great importance for the understanding of what has happened there, but this is rarely grasped by foreign observers. . . . That in Germany it was the Jew who became the enemy until his place was taken by the "plutocracies" was no less a result of the anticapitalist resentment on which the whole movement was based than the selection of the kulak in Russia.[67]

Without mentioning the Jews explicitly, Hayek explored their fate in his major postwar work, *The Constitution of Liberty* (1960):

There can be little question that, from the point of view of society, the art of turning one's capacity to good account, the skill of discovering the most effective use of one's gift, is perhaps the most useful of all; but too much resourcefulness of this kind is not uncommonly frowned upon, and an advantage gained over those of equal general capacity by a more successful exploitation of concrete circumstances is regarded as unfair. In many societies an "aristocratic" tradition that stems from the conditions of action in an organizational hierarchy with assigned tasks and duties, a tradition that has often been developed by people whose privileges have freed them from the necessity of giving others what they want, represent it as nobler to wait until one's gifts are discovered by others, while only religious or ethnic minorities in a hard struggle to rise have deliberately cultivated this kind of resourcefulness (best described by the German term *Findigkeit*)—and are generally disliked for that reason. Yet there can be no doubt that the discovery of a better use of things or of one's own capacities is one of the greatest contributions that an individual can make in our society to the welfare of his fellows and that it is by providing the maximum opportunity for this that a free society can become so much more prosperous than others. The successful use of this entrepreneurial capacity (and, in discovering the best use of our abilities, we are all entrepreneurs) is the most highly rewarded activity in a free society, while whoever leaves to others the task of finding some useful means of employing his capacities must be content with a smaller reward.[68]

Capitalism, as Hayek conceived it, was fundamentally dynamic, and that dynamism was due to the discovery of new needs and new ways of fulfilling them by entrepreneurs possessed with "resourcefulness."

That economic vibrancy created a social and cultural dynamic, demanding the adaptation of old ways of thinking and behaving. The dynamic and resourceful few forced the less resourceful many to adapt, to rationalize their behavior by imitating the more successful. This process was sometimes painful, as Hayek noted in his seminal essay of 1968, "Competition as a Discovery Procedure," and bound to be resented by those who preferred to run in the well-wrought grooves of established ways of life. For the

> required changes in habits and customs will be brought about only if the few willing and able to experiment with new methods can make it necessary for the many to follow them, and at the same time to show them the way. The required discovery process will be impeded or prevented, if the many are able to keep the few to the traditional ways. Of course, it is one of the chief reasons for the

dislike of competition that it not only shows how things can be done more effectively, but also confronts those who depend for their incomes on the market with the alternative of imitating the more successful or losing some or all of their income.[69]

For Hayek, the Jews were merely the most striking example of those whose resourcefulness led to the creative destruction so characteristic of competitive capitalism. Once again, the Jews are linked to capitalism: but for Hayek, as for Montesquieu, this is a positive linkage. The Jews are valued precisely for demonstrating the cultural trait of resourcefulness, the *intellectual* act of discovering new opportunities for the use of resources. This is a variety of work that does not require the sweat of the brow, but is a form of productive labor, perhaps the quintessential form of productive labor under capitalism.

The fall of Nazism and Communism did not bring the anticommercial and antifinancial rhetoric of usury to an end. Its echoes could still be heard early in the twenty-first century in the rhetoric of accusation against the World Bank and the International Monetary Fund. Since the end of Communism, the condemnation of capitalism, Jewry, and the United States have frequently been blended to-gether, with the shadow of usury and the specter of the Jews now cast over the United States.[70] It also forms a recurrent theme in the pronouncements of Osama Bin Laden, as in his "Letter to America" of November 2002:

> You are the nation that permits Usury, which has been forbidden by all the religions. Yet you build your economy and investments on Usury. As a result of this, in all its different forms and guises, the Jews have taken control of your economy, through which they have then taken control of your media, and now control all aspects of your life making you their servants and achieving their aims at your expense.[71]

Tracing the long shadow of usury casts an unexpected light on the history of thinking about capitalism, and about the Jews. For better and for worse, the image of the Jew and the evaluation of capitalism have been deeply intertwined.

CHAPTER TWO

The Jewish Response to Capitalism
Milton Friedman's Paradox Reconsidered

In a lecture first delivered in 1972 entitled "Capitalism and the Jews," Milton Friedman, the distinguished libertarian economist and defender of the free market, presented what he regarded as a paradox: the Jews "owe an enormous debt to free enterprise and competitive capitalism," but "for at least the past century the Jews have been consistently opposed to capitalism and have done much on an ideological level to undermine it."[1]

Friedman argued that the element of capitalism that has most benefited the Jews is free competition. Free competition counteracts the forces of anti-Semitic prejudice. For under conditions of free competition, ethnic or religious discrimination puts the discriminator at a competitive disadvantage. The customer who buys from the baker that shares his race, or ideology, or religion, rather than from the baker who produces the best bread at the cheapest price, pays a premium. The law firm that hires only lawyers of the traditionally dominant ethnic group eventually finds itself losing more cases and more clients to firms who hire the best and brightest lawyers, regardless of origin. The use of such discriminatory criteria, Friedman argued, is most likely to occur under conditions of monopoly, governmental or private, where the quest for comparative economic advantage is less acute. In a more competitive market, by contrast, prejudice becomes more disadvantageous. Hiring the less qualified, or buying from the less efficient producer because buyer and seller share some cultural trait, will eventually lead to bankruptcy.

That Jews have benefited from capitalism is difficult to dispute, in good part for the reason advanced by Friedman. Yet not all minorities long subject to discrimination necessarily succeed under conditions of market competition. Jews did do disproportionately well, but for reasons that Friedman did not bother to explore. That is the subject of the first half of this essay, after which it turns to Friedman's claim about Jews as ideological opponents of capitalism. As we will see, that claim is a half-truth at best, hiding the fact that Jewish voters have tended to support procapitalist parties and that

Jewish intellectuals have often embraced capitalism as a boon not only for the Jews, but for society at large. Still, Friedman's contention about Jewish antipathy to capitalism has an element of truth, even if it mistakes a limited slice of historical reality for the larger whole.

First we must dispose of two definitional issues: What do we mean by capitalism? And what do we mean by "the Jews"?

To give a working definition, capitalism is a social system in which most economic activity is coordinated through the market, using the mechanism of prices, based on competition, and employing free labor. This definition is an ideal type: in the real world, such a social system has existed with elements of unfree labor and with a substantial role for government in the coordination of economic activity. One element that is particularly important for thinking about the fate of Jews under capitalism is legal equality, in which entry into businesses and occupations is not restricted by the law of the land. The fact that it might remain restricted by social custom, as we will see, was a factor in accounting for the occupational choices that Jews made. But in the long run, legal equality along with a competitive market tends to erode the influence of discrimination by social custom.

When thinking about Jews and capitalism, what do we mean by "Jews"? Here we face a perennial problem. Should we define as Jews those of Jewish lineage who converted or otherwise distanced themselves from Jewish identification? Should we include only those who considered *themselves* Jews? Or should we consider all those regarded as Jews by *others*? It is impossible to give a single answer: the criteria that we use will depend upon the historical problem under investigation. But whatever criterion we apply, we ought to apply it consistently. In thinking about the fate of Jews under capitalism, it is probably more useful to consider not only those who identified as Jews, but also those who converted to Christianity, or to some secular form of identity meant to divorce them from identification as Jews, at least for a few generations after their departure from the Jewish fold. Such a criterion makes sense for two reasons. First, because in most European societies, Jewish converts and their immediate descendents were still regarded as in some sense "Jewish" by the larger society. Second, because to the extent that we are interested, as we will be, in the transmission of cultural traits from generation to generation, it makes little sense to assume that such transmission ceased with conversion.

Historians have become sensitive to the dangers of "essentializing." That sensitivity is useful when it reminds us of the error of treating group characterizations that are the *product* of history (such as business acumen) as if they were the *source* of historical development. But the fear of essentializing becomes counterproductive when it leads to the avoidance of all generalization, leaving only a collection of particular cases. Our quest is for useful generalizations: that is, for generalizations that hold up much, though not all, of the time.

In considering the response of Jews to capitalism we can look either at their ideologically articulated formulations, or at what economists call "revealed preferences." The notion of revealed preferences is that we discover what people want not from what individuals *say* but from what they *do*. Let us begin with these revealed preferences, that is, with the *actions* of Jews as opposed to their ideologies, religious and secular. Or, as Karl Marx put it, "Let us consider the actual, worldly Jew." Then we will turn to more intellectual and ideological responses, what Marx called the "Sabbath Jew"—

a subject of interest to us, though it was of no concern to Marx.

As the development of modern capitalism created new economic opportunities in Europe and its colonial offshoots, Jews were disproportionately successful at seizing them. That is because the Jews of Europe were well positioned by their premodern history. Their experience, and the cultural propensities it engendered, predisposed them toward commerce and finance, and toward the free professions.

Jewish Demography in the Transition to Capitalism

At the beginning of the modern period, around 1700, just over half of the Jews in the world lived in eastern Europe. Of the 1,100,000 Jews then living, 370,000 lived in Asia and North Africa, 146,000 lived in central and western Europe, while 570,000 lived in eastern Europe and the Balkans.[2] Spain, which had been a center of Jewish life in the medieval era, ceased to be one with the expulsion of the Jews at the end of the fifteenth century, followed by their expulsion from Portugal. During the sixteenth and seventeenth centuries, large numbers of

Jews settled in the Polish-Lithuanian Commonwealth, which became the demographic and cultural center of world Jewry. As a result of the partition of Poland in the late eighteenth century, the Jews of eastern Europe were divided among Prussia, the Habsburg empire, and above all the Romanov empire. There, most Jews were restricted to living in the so-called Pale of Settlement, the westernmost area of Russia between the Baltic and Black seas, where they comprised a substantial portion of the urban population. For the most part, Jews were legally confined to this backward economic region, and only a handful were permitted to live and work in the regions of the empire where economic opportunity was greater.[3]

In the course of the nineteenth century, the Jews of eastern Europe (including Ukraine, White Russia, Lithuania, Poland, Romania, Galicia, and Hungary) experienced one of the most rapid population increases in all of Europe, when their number grew from about 1.5 million at the beginning of the century to almost eight million by 1913 (two million of whom emigrated to the New World). While demographic growth occurred throughout Europe, the Jews' rate of growth outstripped that of their non-Jewish counterparts. That is not because Jewish birthrates went up, but because their mortality rates went down, and did so several decades before their gentile neighbors. Both cultural factors in family-life and child-rearing practices, and the greater orientation of Jews to the use of modern medicine, contributed to this early decline in Jewish mortality rates.[4]

Before this population explosion, most Jews had made their living through one or another form of trade or commerce, from petty trade and tavern keeping to leasing and managing the lands owned by the nobility.[5] The rapid expansion of their numbers made that impossible, and in the course of the nineteenth and early twentieth centuries, the Jews of the Pale went through a process sometimes called *proletarianization*. The term is somewhat misleading, insofar as it implies that they became industrial factory workers. Actually, most became semiskilled handicraft workers, often in small workshops owned by other Jews. By the end of the century, fewer than 40 percent of Jews were engaged in trade or commerce, with an equal number working in manufacture.[6] Those who on ideological grounds viewed commerce as unproductive hailed this movement as a shift to more "productive" occupations. But the Jewish move out of commerce was created by the force of circumstances: by the drastic limitation of economic possibilities that were open to a burgeoning Jewish population, constrained by laws that confined them not merely to the Pale, but more restrictively to urban areas within it. Most of the Jewish population of the Pale was poor, and eked out a living in economic pursuits with low levels of productivity, whether in trade, as handicraft workers, or as unskilled laborers in personal services.[7] Many worked as tailors in tiny establishments.[8] No wonder that eastern Europe became the crucible of Jewish socialism, for the prospects of improvement under capitalism seemed hopeless. And, as we will see in the second half of this essay, the question of what to do with these Jews would prove to be a focus of Jewish ideology as well as of Jewish philanthropy.

This population explosion, together with the restrictions placed on Jews by the Russian authorities and a wave of pogroms after 1880, created enormous incentives for emigration. By 1914, 2.5 million Jews from the Romanov and Habsburg empires had emigrated, with most going to the United States and a smaller number to the countries of western Europe and Latin America.

In the great wave of Jewish migration from eastern Europe after 1880, the largest number settled in New York City. There, two-thirds of the immigrants were employed in the clothing trade. Jewish immigrants came with even less capital than most turn-of-the-century immigrants; they went into an industry with the worst working conditions and with low wages. Yet a substantial number of first-generation immigrants moved from the ranks of workers to entrepreneurs, first in the clothing trades, and then beyond. By the second generation, they had moved into other forms of retailing, and then into real estate and the professions.[9] As laborers, Jews were active in trade unions, but they did not think of themselves as part of a transgenerational working class: on the contrary, they wanted something different, for themselves if possible, and certainly for their children. During the era from 1880 through the 1920s, when a high percentage of Jewish immigrants in America were employed in the needle trades, one of the most striking phenomena was their high rate of mobility from hourly and piecework into management and entrepreneurship.[10] Compared to most immigrant groups, and indeed to most native Americans, they had an abundance of commercial skills, drawn either from their own experience in commerce or from sustained contact with businessmen.[11]

In many regions of the United States, Jews

began as peddlers, the lowest rung on the entrepreneurial ladder, and then moved up to shop-owning and other forms of retailing, before they too made the transition to real estate and the professions.[12] In thinking about Jewish economic success across generations, an important factor was that Jews were not inclined to maintain the economic status quo in a particular inherited craft, but rather to find market opportunities in a changing dynamic economy. For economic success depends not only on a sensitivity to where economic possibilities are opening up, but also on the willingness to abandon a declining economic sector. Jewish economic success across generations was predicated on a readiness to leave the clothing business behind as its potential decreased.[13]

Thus, by the early decades of the twentieth century, Jews had returned to the disproportionate involvement in trade and commerce that had been their pattern from the High Middle Ages through the early nineteenth century.[14]

Premodern Experience and Cultural Dispositions

Jews have had a preference for market-oriented occupations going back to the Middle Ages.

Historians debate how much emphasis to place on factors that pushed Jews out of other economic activities—such as farming and artisanry, from which they were largely excluded by the church and by the religious nature of artisanal guilds—and into commerce and the stigmatized domain of moneylending, and how much on Jewish preferences for commerce.[15] In any case, most Jews retained these commercial propensities into the modern period, adding a taste for the free professions based on education.

Compared to Christianity, Judaism was more favorably disposed toward commerce. To be sure, we cannot derive actual Jewish economic behavior from rabbinical sources. The law of the Talmudic period was intended for a largely self-sufficient Jewish community. Because the biblical and Talmudic economy was oriented above all to the maintenance of a holy covenanted community, the Talmud discouraged economic relations with gentiles.[16] But as the Jews increasingly became a diasporic people, dependent for many functions on the larger population around them, Jewish law was made to adjust.[17] Jews sometimes ignored those sources when they conflicted with perceived economic necessities (as their Christian counterparts did in regard to canon law). And innovations in

Jewish religious law often *followed* changes in practice, such as the legitimation of the taking of interest through the *heter iska*, a legal fiction that disguised loans as investments in a business partnership.[18]

Still, some broad generalizations seem valid enough. Talmudic law—which educated Jews continued to study and refine through the ages—was replete with debates about economic matters, including contracts, torts, and prices. Unlike Christianity, Judaism considered poverty as anything but ennobling. "Nothing is harder to bear than poverty," says the Talmud, "because he who is crushed by poverty is like to one to whom all the troubles of the world cling and upon whom all the curses of Deuteronomy have descended. If all other troubles were placed on one side and poverty on the other, poverty would outweigh them all."[19]

The more favorable Jewish valuation of commerce, compared to Christianity, was due in part to the more favorable Jewish attitude toward the natural passions, which involved a greater emphasis on family and marriage as well. As opposed to the Augustinian view of original sin as the basis of concupiscence (sexual lust), the Talmud, in a famous passage, speaks of "the evil inclination," the *yetzer hara* as the basis of both family and commerce.[20]

Commerce, then, like marriage, was natural and providential.

The rabbis had an acute appreciation of the benefits of the division of labor, as indicated in this tale from the Babylonian Talmud that recalls the early chapters of Adam Smith's *Wealth of Nations*:

Ben Zoma once saw a crowd on one of the steps of the Temple Mount. He said, Blessed is He that discerneth secrets, and blessed is He who has created all these to serve me. [For] he used to say: What labors Adam had to carry out before he obtained bread to eat! He ploughed, he sowed, he reaped, he bound [the sheaves], he threshed and winnowed and selected the ears, he ground [them], and sifted [the flour], he kneaded and baked, and then at last he ate; whereas I get up, and find all these things done for me.

And how many labors Adam had to carry out before he obtained a garment to wear! He had to shear, wash [the wool], comb it, spin it, and weave it, and then at last he obtained a garment to wear; whereas I get up and find all these things done for me. All kinds of craftsmen come early to the door of my house, and I rise in the morning and find all these before me.[21]

This influential body of Jewish religious thought reflected a very different social milieu from which Jewish scholars were drawn, compared to their Christian counterparts. As the Catholic theologian Michael Novak has rightly noted, "Jewish thought has had a candid orientation toward private property, commercial activity, markets, and profits, whereas Catholic thought—articulated from an early period chiefly among priests and monks—has persistently tried to direct the attention of its adherents beyond the activities and interests of this world to the next."[22] Talmudic and halachic legal debates concerning commercial activity shaped the minds of generations of Jewish men, all of whom were expected to study the Talmud to the extent possible.

If Jews did not glorify poverty, neither did they sanctify the attainment of wealth or value physical labor for its own sake. The great halachists (rabbinical authorities) called on men to devote as little time as possible to their occupation, in order to devote more time to study. They therefore preferred commerce to crafts, on the grounds that it was less time-consuming.[23] The suspicion of merchants and commerce so prominent in the Christian tradition was lacking among Jews.[24]

In premodern European societies, Jews were

outside the feudal order of serfs, landowning gentry, and merchants and artisans organized into exclusive guilds. The roles they assumed were largely those of middlemen between producers and consumers: a commercial ladder ranging from peddling and hawking (selling from a horse and cart), through pawnbroking and moneylending, through interregional and international trade. Jews thus formed what might be called a proto-bourgeoisie. Worldly survival meant the ability to cultivate a rational economic ethos, based on maximizing profitability, assessing risk, exploring new markets, and minimizing consumption to maximize the accumulation of capital.[25]

Another part of their cultural ethos was what the sociologist Victor Karady has dubbed "religious intellectualism." Theirs was a religion oriented to continuous contact with texts: a culture of handling books, reading them, and reflecting upon their messages. It was a culture that cultivated the habit of finding commonalities and distinctions in arguments, and of thinking in abstractions. It was a culture that prized the ability to make oral arguments. These cultural traits were easily transferred from religious to secular learning, from holy writ to legal and medical texts, from the yeshiva to the court of law. No wonder then that when the learned professions were opened to them, Jews excelled in fields such as medicine and law.[26]

Moreover, traditional Jewish religious culture fostered cultural traits that stood the Jews in good stead as they entered capitalist societies. The life of *mitzvot* (commandments) meant a style of life based on discipline, on the conscious planning of action, and the avoidance of alcoholic dissipation (intoxication being regarded as a mark of the gentile). Jews came from a culture that favored the nonviolent resolution of conflict, and that valued intellectual over physical prowess.[27]

All of this was a recipe for what economists now call "cultural capital." Jews had the behavioral traits conducive to success in a capitalist society. They entered commercializing societies with a stock of know-how from their families and communities about how markets work, about calculating profit and loss, about assessing and taking risks.[28] Most important, though hardest to specify, Jews demonstrated a propensity for discovering new wants and to bringing underused resources to the market.

Jewish success in the market was also based upon longer time horizons. Jews typically entered businesses at the bottom rung of the commercial ladder, such as peddling and shopkeeping. These required little capital to enter, but that in turn meant that with few barriers to entry, competition was plentiful. Success in such endeavors required a willingness to work long and hard and to save in order to accumulate capital. All of this was worthwhile only on the assumption that gratification would come in the long run: perhaps, indeed, in the next generation. Jews had long prized religious education, with the yeshiva scholar a source of familial pride. When universities opened their doors to Jews, that cultural preference was transmuted into a high valuation of secular education. The high Jewish valuation of secular education also reflected a long time horizon, in which the economic payoff would be deferred for years. The cultural emphasis on educational effort and educational success was of course conducive to movement into the professions.[29]

Jews, then, were more than just a community of traders. Rather, they took the cultural propensities that had developed out of centuries of experience as a merchant minority, and that were transmitted from generation to generation, and applied them to a variety of sectors: as agricultural estate managers in eastern Europe; as provisioners of governments in central Europe; as manufacturers of textiles and of much else in western Europe and the United States; and as the creators of new industries of mass entertainment, from books through movies and recorded music.[30] Thus, as one student of the subject has aptly put it, the Jews' historical experience predisposed them "to independence and self-sufficiency since they lived in a hostile or indifferent society; to professionalism, where practice was as important as profits; to scholarly pursuits, where long preparation meant a lengthy postponement of gratification; to progressive industries, where innovation was rewarded; and to peripheral enterprises, which allowed for expansion without direct competition with basic and mainstream corporations."[31]

There were also Jews who applied their entrepreneurial virtues to vice—to "peripheral enterprises" that were on the border of the licit, or beyond. In the late nineteenth and early twentieth centuries, the extreme poverty of eastern European Jewry together with international migration led to substantial networks of Jews engaged in sexual commerce (as pimps, prostitutes, and brothel owners), a phenomenon that appalled established Jewish communities in Germany, Austria, Britain and the United States, and led them to mobilize organizationally to stamp out the phenomenon.[32] During the era of Prohibition in the United

States, Jews were disproportionately active in the trade in illicit booze. The most successful Jewish gangsters then invested their profits in the gambling industry and played a seminal role in the creation of Las Vegas, that quintessential site of American vice cum mass entertainment.[33]

Another factor that explains Jewish economic success was the propensity to develop social networks. These overlapping personal connections were more readily fostered by Jews, who by virtue of their religion were subject to prejudice and exclusion by the larger, gentile society, and who felt a sense of community and commonality with other Jews, whether from shared religious commitment, or common culture, or involuntarily shared fate. The obligation to look after fellow Jews was deeply embedded in Jewish law and culture, and it existed not just in theory but in practice. It took a variety of forms, from simple charity, to mutual aid societies offering low-cost loans to newcomers, to the sharing of information about potential commercial opportunities. Over and above religious obligation and cultural affinity was the awareness that in a society in which Jews were a stigmatized minority, all Jews were judged by the actions of the least successful or respectable, adding self-interest to the motives for mutual aid.[34]

Social networks were made possible, then, by a sense of commonality—of shared culture, shared fate, and shared responsibility. As with other diasporic merchant minorities, social networks induced trust across wide distances. Jewish merchants who acquired a reputation for dishonesty or unreliability in business would be ostracized by their own communities, thus providing a form of collective self-policing. To the extent that Jews in other communities were made aware of who was reliable and who was not, the risks of conducting business were reduced.[35] A shared language—whether Hebrew, Spanish, Ladino, or Yiddish—also facilitated interregional and international trade. The classic example was the Spanish-Jewish diaspora, which provided many of the links that connected the commerce of the early modern world, links stretching from Europe, to Turkey, to the New World, and beyond, trading goods such as sugar, tobacco, coffee, and diamonds.[36]

Another cultural trait affecting the Jewish response to capitalism was the propensity to high familial investment in children. Long before the term *human capital* was coined, Jews were investing heavily in it. The care and attention lavished upon Jewish children by Jewish mothers was a cultural stereotype, which, like many stereotypes, reflected an underlying reality. In the nineteenth century, that attention was in part responsible for the fact that as we have seen, in eastern Europe, Jewish mortality rates fell sooner and faster than elsewhere. Later on, this emphasis on human capital formation led Jews to bring down their fertility faster and sooner than most other groups.[37] This pattern was already visible by the turn of the twentieth century among Jews in western and central Europe. In America, working-class Jewish immigrants were distinguished from most of their non-Jewish counterparts by their willingness to forego income from their children's labor, in favor of having children attend school longer or learn trades.[38] This was a communal norm, embraced by the advice column of the Yiddish daily *Forward*, the "Bintel Brief," and commented upon at the time by gentile observers.[39] The willingness to forego current familial income in order to improve the life chances of offspring was therefore reflected in higher levels of educational attendance and educational attainment.[40]

Jewish Economic Success

Jews tended to prosper wherever they attained that civic equality that allowed them to engage freely in market activity. Jews possessed such rights in the United States from the founding of the new nation in 1776, though religious tests for office were retained in some states. In the course of the nineteenth century, Jews were granted civic equality first in the nations of western Europe (Britain and France), and then in the newly created German empire in 1871, and shortly thereafter in the Austria-Hungarian empire. Civic equality in Russia, where the greatest number of Jews lived, came only with the fall of the Romanovs in 1917. Civic equality meant that, legally at least, Jews were able to compete economically with non-Jews on equal terms. In each case, the opening up of opportunity led to disproportionate Jewish economic success, or to put it another way, to a huge increase in Jewish contributions to economic life. And since "economic life" is not a distinct domain, that meant Jewish contributions to, and overrepresentation in, a variety of realms, from trade to medicine to culture. But Jewish economic attainment led to very different degrees of Jewish economic *salience*, depending on the economic capacities and commercial orientations of the larger society. And that in turn led to very different *reactions* to Jewish economic success.

Britain and the United States were already highly commercial societies in the nineteenth century, in which most capitalist development was carried out by non-Jews. These were also societies in which commerce tended to be taken for granted, and anticapitalist sentiments were relatively weak. So in the United States and Britain, Jews could be economically successful without being particularly conspicuous, except in new industries into which Jews moved in search of opportunity, such as the movie business. And in societies that regarded capitalist dynamism as natural and desirable, Jewish economic activity tended to be welcomed.[41] Thus, anti-Semitism in the United States was relatively mild during the first century of the nation's history, and the Jewish immigrants—most of them from German-speaking Europe—reached remarkable levels of commercial success and cultural acceptance. That was true in the North, where a group of German-Jewish banking families formed part of the patriciate of New York City (the Seligmans, Guggenheims, Goldmans, Wertheims), and the merchant princes (Edward Filene and Adam Gimbel among others) came to dominate retailing, particularly department stores.[42] It also held in the West, where a German Jewish immigrant, Levi Strauss, opened a branch of his family's dry goods business in San Francisco at the time of the California gold rush, and then turned to manufacturing the metal-riveted denim pants that still bear his name. And it held in the South, where Judah P. Benjamin, a Jewish lawyer and erstwhile plantation owner, became senator from Louisiana, attorney general of the Confederacy, its secretary of war and finally its secretary of state.

Through most of the history of Jews in America, it was primarily the relatively advantageous conditions created by American economic growth that brought Jews from central and eastern Europe to the United States in large numbers. They came to America's shores motivated not by religion but in spite of it, their more orthodox leaders being inclined to warn them against the dangers of godless and goyish America.[43]

In eastern Europe, by contrast, capitalism was a newer phenomenon. The non-Jewish majority was typically composed of landowners and peasants, neither of them particularly adept at market activity. In these regions, Jews *were* the commercial class, leading to a close identification of capitalism with the Jews. As a result, as Victor Karady has noted, "the high rates of participation by Jews in commerce and finance was the more conspicuous the less highly developed these sectors were in the national economy."[44] Moreover, since jobs in the government sector were usually closed to Jews, they turned to vocations in the competitive market, from commerce and finance to the classic professions of law, medicine, and engineering.[45]

Germany fell in between the western European and eastern European pattern. There, Jews played an important role in capitalist development, but alongside a dominant Christian (mostly Protestant) capitalist class.

It was in central Europe, across the German and Austria-Hungarian empires that Jewish economic success was most conspicuous from the mid-nineteenth century through the rise of National Socialism. It is a useful simplification to think of modern European societies as located along a civilizational gradient, running from west to east, from the Atlantic coast to the Russian steppes.[46] On the western side of this gradient, states tended to be more ethnically homogeneous at the beginning of the modern age, governments exercised more effective control over their inhabitants, civil society was more developed, commerce was more advanced, and civil equality came earlier to minorities, including to the Jews. As one moved eastward, territories contained more mixed populations, government authority was weaker and more fragmented, commerce and civil society were less developed. Civic equality began to be extended to the Jews on the western end of the gradient during the era of the French Revolution, and reached the eastern end of the gradient only with the February revolution of 1917.[47]

The fact that Jews were relatively few in number in the nations along the western end of the gradient (Britain, France, Holland) may have been a factor in easing their way to citizenship and in limiting the vehemence of anti-Semitism. But it also meant that their impact on the larger society was more limited. In Russia, on the eastern end of the gradient, there were more Jews, living in greater concentration. But while Jews did play a substantial role in the economic modernization of nineteenth-century Russia,[48] the relative economic backwardness of the region limited their economic prospects.

It was in the middle of the gradient, in Germany and in Austria-Hungary, that Jewish economic and cultural mobility was most marked. For there, in the decades of the mid-nineteenth century, Jews in substantial numbers were emancipated in societies undergoing rapid capitalist development. By the turn of the century, Jews, who constituted about 4 percent of the inhabitants of Berlin, paid 30 percent of the municipal taxes in the German capital.[49]

Jews famously played a key role in nineteenth-century banking. Foremost among merchant banks (which lent out their own capital) was the house of Rothschild, with branches in Frankfurt, London, Paris, Vienna, and Naples. Close on their heels were the Bleichröders in Berlin and the house of Oppenheim in Cologne.[50] Perhaps more important was the role of Jews in founding the great joint stock or commercial banks, which mobilized capital from thousands of depositors and played an indispensable role in capitalist economic development. Jews helped to establish two of the three largest German banks of this sort, the Deutsche Bank and the Dresdner Bank, as well as their French counterpart, the Crédit Mobilier.[51]

In Germany on the eve of World War I, about half the Jewish working population was involved in commerce, trade, and finance, and the percentages in the Austro-Hungarian monarchy were similar.[52] Within that sector, Jews were moving rapidly from the lowest to the highest rungs.[53] Werner Mosse's study of the

German corporate elite on the eve of World War I found that Jews comprised 32–40 percent, most of whom made their money in commerce or finance.[54] By the 1920s, 54 percent of owners of commercial establishments in Hungary were Jews, and Jews comprised 85 percent of the bank directors and owners of the country's financial institutions. Despite the obstacles placed in their path in Russia, Jews played a disproportionate role in the organization and ownership of major Russian industries, including textiles, sugar refining, flour mills, sawmills, grain and timber, banking, transport, and mining. According to the Russian economist M. Bernatsky, by 1916 Jews constituted 35 percent of the Russian mercantile class. Jews also comprised much of the entrepreneurial class in interwar Poland.[55]

No group was more committed to acquiring higher education and the professional occupations that higher education made possible. In the late nineteenth century, Jews were radically overrepresented in institutions of elite education: by a factor of ten in Prussia, five in Austria, six in Hungary and Bohemia-Moravia.[56] By the early twentieth century, especially in the capitals and larger cities of central and eastern Europe, such as Vienna, Warsaw, Prague, or Budapest, Jewish lawyers, engineers, pharmacists, and architects at times comprised the majority of practitioners, in cities where Jews generally made up 5 to 10 percent of the population.[57]

If Jewish economic performance in central Europe in the late nineteenth and early twentieth centuries was striking, Jewish economic success in the United States would eventually become equally remarkable. Jews moved quickly out of manual labor, in which many first-generation immigrants had been engaged, and into proprietorship, management, and professional and technical fields. By the 1970s, about 70 percent of Jewish men could be found in these sectors, over twice the proportion of the general population.[58] By the early 1980s, when *Forbes* magazine began to compile its annual list of the four hundred richest Americans, Jews were conspicuously overrepresented. While comprising about 3 percent of the population, they made up a quarter of the names on the list. The largest fortunes, by and large, were made in real estate, an area of the economy that provided some of the greatest opportunity.[59]

Large established corporations had long discriminated against promotion of Jews into their executive ranks. And Jews, in turn, had avoided bureaucratic corporations where promotion often depended on the evaluation of superiors whose judgment might be tinged with anti-Jewish prejudice. It was a symbolic turning point, therefore, when the venerable Dupont Corporation appointed a Jew, Irving Shapiro, as its president in 1973, indicative of the waning of anti-Semitism in corporate America. But in general, Jews continued to prefer self-employment, whether as owners of manufacturing and retailing firms, or as professionals.[60]

As had been the case in central Europe, Jews in the United States were astonishingly oriented to higher education. By the mid-1970s, when just under half of Americans went on to college, 80 percent of Jews did. They were disproportionately represented among students at prestigious universities. And, in a distinct break from the European and American past, they came to be heavily represented on the faculties of American universities, including the most prestigious, comprising one-fifth of the faculty of elite universities and one-quarter of the faculty of the Ivy League.[61] While these schools had maintained quotas on the admission of Jews until after World War II, by the last decades of the century, Jews were increasingly becoming the presidents of Ivy League universities.

It is no surprise perhaps that Jews have been particularly conspicuous in the field of economic science, where commerce and academic learning meet. In the thirty-eight years the Nobel Prize for economics was awarded from its inception in 1970 until 2008, the award went to an economist of Jewish origin twenty-two times.

So, Friedman was right. In an economic sense, and in the long run, capitalism was good for the Jews. And the Jews were good for capitalism. As Simon Kuznets, winner of the 1971 Nobel Prize for economics once noted:

> Given the kind of human capital that the Jews represent, the majority in any country, if it wished to maximize long-term economic returns, should have not only permitted the Jewish minority the utmost freedom, but in fact should have subsidized any improvement in the economic and social performance of promising individual Jews. Such help in developing contributors to the stock of human knowledge and hence to economic capacity would have been a high-yield investment. If only for this reason, the discriminatory policies of many majorities, often specifically retarding the dynamics of Jewish minorities—from trade into intellectual and professional pursuits, within business corporations, etc.—constitute extreme economic irrationality.[62]

Political and Ideological Responses

Let us turn from revealed preferences to the level of articulated ideologies.

Before addressing the issue of Jewish ideological responses to capitalism, it is worth recalling the range of Jewish *political* responses to modernity. For the sake of analysis, one can group them under four broad rubrics: integrationist, isolationist, socialist, and nationalist. There were, of course, Jews who responded to the promise of civil equality by attempting to assimilate completely into the nations in which they lived, to the point of conversion to Christianity or otherwise abandoning all ties to Judaism through conversion (for such it was) to the Communist faith. But the path chosen by the majority of Jews, as the historian Ezra Mendelsohn has recently noted, is best termed *integrationist*. Jewish integrationists sought to become part of the larger society without giving up a distinct Jewish identity. That often entailed adoption of the national language, a reform of the Jewish religion, and the redefinition of Judaism as simply a religion, without a national element.[63] This was the path of Jewish liberalism, and it usually coincided with an embrace of capitalism in the economic realm.

The term *isolationist* refers to those who

sought to maintain the traditional community intact to the extent possible, to resist modernity and reform in principle, and to engage in politics only to the extent necessary to protect the fortunes of the orthodox Jewish community. This was the path typified by ultraorthodoxy and its political manifestation, *Agudat Yisrael* (The League of Israel). Perhaps its best-known instance in the United States is the Satmar Hasidim, who have gone so far as to found their own town in Orange County, New York, Kiryas Joel, named after their late rebbe, Joel Teitelbaum. The isolationist camp had no articulated view of economic matters. Entirely antipathetic to socialism, its adherents typically sought niches in the capitalist economy that would minimize social contact with gentiles and with less orthodox Jews. In both the state of Israel and the United States, such communities often draw heavily upon governmental welfare payments, which they use to subsidize a style of life focused on the study of Talmud by men, high levels of childbearing by women, and low levels of secular education and economic achievement.[64]

There were Jewish *socialists* of many varieties. They disagreed with one another about what elements of Jewish culture ought to be preserved (typically, but not always, the Yiddish language), but had in common a commitment to the replacement of capitalism by socialism.

And there were varieties of *Zionists*, who disagreed with one another about the desired economy of the Jewish society they sought to create, but who agreed on the need for a distinct territory over which Jews would exercise sovereign power.

Most Jews in western and central Europe and in the United States tended toward one or another version of integrationism (though some who favored integrationism in their own societies regarded it as impossible in the more ethnically national states of eastern Europe, and favored a nationalist solution for the Jews of eastern Europe).[65] Integrationism typically went together with a favorable attitude toward capitalism: after all, legal equality of entry into business and the professions was one of the most attractive elements of the liberal societies into which Jews sought to integrate.

Is it true, as Milton Friedman claimed, that Jews tended to be ideologically opposed to capitalism? Friedman's contention that "for at least the past century the Jews have been consistently opposed to capitalism and have done much on an ideological level to undermine it" is at best a half-truth, which recent scholarship has gone a long way to discredit. To buttress his contention, Friedman pointed to the overrepresentation of Jews in Communist parties (the subject of the next essay in this volume). But most of his argument rested on the propensity of Jews in western democratic societies to vote for left-of-center parties.

Friedman rightly attributed this phenomenon in part to the tendency of the parties of the right to define citizenship in integralist terms: that is, to regard one or another form of Christianity as a prerequisite of citizenship. To the extent that this was the motivation for Jews to eschew parties of the Right, it is hardly evidence of anticapitalism. Most Jews in Austria-Hungary, Germany, France, or Britain in fact voted for liberal parties, in the European sense, that is, for parties that were laicist, but not anticapitalist.[66]

There were indeed many Jews who identified with socialism. They often did so for the same reasons that non-Jews were drawn toward the movement: out of a sense that capitalism was unfair and that collective ownership of the means of production would be more rational and productive than the purported "anarchy" of the market. But seen historically, the identification of Jews with socialism was more fortuitous and fleeting than it might at first appear. It is a true but historically contingent fact that socialism was popular among Jews—especially, but not exclusively, with working-class Jews—in Russia in the late nineteenth and early twentieth centuries. That was in good part because at the time the socialists were the only mass movement that offered Jews the prospect of equal citizenship and social acceptance. In the decades after 1880, wave upon wave of Jewish immigrants brought these propensities with them, not only to the United States, but also to France, Britain, Canada, and to the Land of Israel.[67] Often enough the first generation of immigrant Jews, facing social discrimination, wretched working conditions, and poverty, looked to socialism as an alternative, one that promised a neutral ground where Jew and gentile could meet as equals. As an alternative to the manifest failings of capitalism, socialism was all the more plausible to the extent that it was untried. Some Jewish socialists sought to selectively reconfigure Jewish tradition to presage the socialist future, with a bevy of passages from Isaiah and vague references to the messianic age. But for many, socialism represented a break with the Jewish past, an escape from the social and intellectual world of the ghetto into a world of postethnic comradeship: the brotherhood of man.[68]

The result was a left-wing politics that put the immigrant Jews, and often their children, at odds with the politics of the native born—Jewish and non-Jewish alike. Yet with each succeeding generation, the hold of socialism became weaker. In the United States, it ended as a political force in the era of the New Deal.[69] Socialism lived on in intellectual life, less as a program than as organized nostalgia and as a form of secular ethnic identification. It is no coincidence that Irving Howe, who founded the socialist journal *Dissent* in 1954, was also the author of the nostalgic *World of Our Fathers*—a volume on the American Jewish immigrant experience that systematically played down the alacrity and rapidity with which Jews moved into American business.[70]

If we broaden our perspective to take in the almost four centuries of modern Jewish history in the diverse nations of the West, a different picture emerges. We find that from the seventeenth century onward, Jewish intellectuals often argued in favor of commerce and capitalism. Intellectual leaders of the Jewish community argued that Jews had an affinity for capitalism, and that conditions of freer competition would allow such talents to redound to the common good. And Jewish writers made important contributions to explaining and understand-

ing the capitalist economy three centuries before the establishment of a Nobel Prize for
economics.

In the seventeenth and eighteenth centuries,
when Jews were excluded from residence in
many parts of Europe, Jewish spokesmen plead-
ed for toleration of the Jews on the grounds of
the economic benefits they would bring. They
argued that commerce was beneficial to the
larger community, they explained the utility of
money and credit, and they pointed to the
unique mercantile qualifications of the Jews.[71]
In 1638, when the Jews of Venice were threatened by expulsion, the Venetian rabbi, Simone
Luzzatto, penned his *Discourse on the Condition
of the Jews and Particularly Those Residing in the
City of Venice*. He argued that Jews were ideally
suited to perform the role of a nation's commercial agents, since they possessed trading
skills honed over centuries by their exclusion
from other sources of livelihood.[72] This line of
argument was picked up a few years later by
Menasseh ben Israel, a Sephardic rabbi from
Amsterdam, who in 1655 petitioned the government of Oliver Cromwell to readmit the
Jews into England. Menasseh pointed to the
advantages of admitting the Jews, including
their knowledge of trade and finance and their
international commercial connections. "Mer-

chandizing is, as it were, the proper profession of the Nation of the Jews," he contended, explaining that the Jewish talent for commerce was providential. For God had implanted a commercial talent in the Jews in order to make them indispensable to the gentile nations that would host and protect them during their long exile.[73]

These were arguments appropriate for societies in which trade was regarded as a specialized function, to be carried on by a distinct group of people, rather than characteristic of society as a whole. By the eighteenth century, western European societies had become more fully commercialized, and it was possible to speak, as Adam Smith did in *The Wealth of Nations*, of societies in which "every man . . . lives by exchanging, and becomes in some measure a merchant." The great Jewish philosopher of the Enlightenment, Moses Mendelssohn, made a more sweeping argument, tying the argument for Jewish toleration to wider reflections on the utility of commerce and the defense of free trade. Mendelssohn—who earned his living as a merchant—argued that the traditional commercial occupations of the Jews were genuinely beneficial to society at large. The popular notion that commerce and trade were less useful or productive than manual labor, Mendelssohn contended, was based on a fundamental misunderstanding.

> Not only *making something* but *doing something* also, is called *producing*. Not he alone who labors with his hands, but generally, whoever does, promotes, occasions, or facilitates anything that may tend to the benefit or comfort of his fellow-creatures, deserves to be called a producer; and, at times, he deserves it the more, the less you see him move his hands or feet. Many a merchant, while quietly engaged at his desk in forming commercial speculations, or pondering, while lolling on his sofa, on distant adventures, produces, in the main, more than the most active and noisy mechanic or tradesman.

Mendelssohn argued against restrictive laws that prevented competition and in favor of a free, competitive market, along the lines suggested by David Hume and Adam Smith.[74] His was a case, not for the Jews as a distinct commercial caste, but for a society characterized by commerce and free competition—for capitalism.

Although the entry of Jews into the mainstream of European and American intellectual life was a relatively late phenomenon, many of the foremost theorists of capitalist activity have been Jews.

In the seventeenth and eighteenth centuries, Jews were still marginal to European society and to European intellectual life. They were hardly devoid of intellectual pursuits, but the Talmudic reflections of the Vilna Gaon or the spiritual doctrines of the Baal Shem Tov were far removed from the intellectual world of the Enlightenment. Nevertheless, Jews made at least two substantial contributions to early modern economic thought. They came from the ranks of the Sephardic merchants of Amsterdam, perhaps the most economically and intellectually integrated community in early modern Europe. In 1688, Josef Penso de la Vega published (in Spanish) the first treatise on the stock exchange, *Confusion of Confusions: Curious Dialogues Between a Witty Philosopher, a Discrete Merchant, and a Learned Stock Investor*. A century later, in his *Treatise on Circulation and Credit*, published in Amsterdam in 1771, Isaac de Pinto (1717–1787) defended a conception of wealth understood as the maximization of exchange, and provided one of the first systematic defenses of public debt, a key element of the eighteenth-century capitalist economy, and a much disputed one at the time.[75]

As the movement of Jews into the mainstream of cultural life picked up in western and central Europe in the first half of the nineteenth century, their contribution to the analysis and promotion of capitalism grew apace. The greatest economist in the generation after Adam Smith, David Ricardo—to whom we owe the concept of mutual gains from trade based on comparative advantage—was the British-born son of Dutch Sephardic Jews, who left the faith at the age of twenty-one when he married a Quaker woman. To regard Karl Marx as a Jew is in many respects fallacious, as he neither knew much about Judaism nor thought of himself as a Jew, having been baptized a Lutheran as a child. But if Marx is to be counted as evidence of the link between Jewish intellectuals and socialism, surely David Ricardo must weigh as heavily on the other side of the ledger.

The Jewish communities of central and eastern Europe underwent their own process of enlightenment in the late eighteenth and early nineteenth centuries, known as the *Haskalah*, and it too had an economic dimension. The key conflict was not between advocates and opponents of market activity, but between the ideals of textual study and economic activity as such. Writing in Yiddish and Hebrew, enlightened authors (*maskilim*) chastised the rabbinic elites of the Jewish community for emphasizing Talmudic study at the expense of worldly economic action. They contrasted the contemporary rabbinic propensity to channel intellectual energy into a life of full-time study with the rabbis of the Talmudic era, who tended to engage in practical economic pursuits in addition to religious study. The rabbinic alienation from productive work, the *maskilim* maintained, corrupted Jewish character, and drained the Jewish community of resources that ought to be redeployed from rabbinic to vocational education. They engaged in their own reinterpretation of key religious terms and produced a literature of moral exhortation (*musar*) that stressed the virtues of worldly labor. Some *maskilim* regarded the Jewish overrepresentation in petty trade as part of the problem, and tried to orient younger Jews toward agriculture and crafts—an attempt that would be repeated in many variations for the next century and more.[76]

From the mid-nineteenth century until the outbreak of World War I, as Jews in central and western Europe moved into the mainstream of European economic and cultural life, discussions among Jews about their relationship to capitalism were more likely to be celebratory than antipathetic. Jewish writers drew a positive link between Jews, trade, and economic freedom, and speculated proudly on sources of Jewish economic success. The editors of the leading newspapers of German-speaking Jewry, the Viennese Jewish weekly *Die Neuzeit* (The Modern Age) and the *Allgemeine Zeitung des Judentums* (The Jewish General Journal) supported economic freedom, saw it as of benefit to the Jews, and stressed the contribution of Jews to economic development through their commercial acumen.[77] In late-nineteenth-century Austria-Hungary, Jews were the most prominent defenders of liberalism, at a time when that ideology came under attack from Catholics, socialists, and Slavic nationalists.[78]

The Jewish response to capitalism was influenced by the repeated claim that trade and commerce were fundamentally unproductive. Recall that in the medieval West, Jews were associated with moneylending—a stigmatized activity permitted them precisely because they were regarded as outside the community of the Christian faithful. Underlying the church's condemnation of moneylenders and suspicion of merchants was the assumption that only those whose work produced sweat really worked and produced. The economic value of gathering and analyzing information went unrecognized, and not only by those who lived off the land or worked with their hands. The notion of trade and of moneylending as unproductive was often expressed in images of parasitism, which continued even when the influence of Christian theology waned. This was the accusation to which Mendelssohn had responded, and much of the traditional accusation was simply reformulated in a new vocabulary in modern socialism. There were intellectuals, such as Karl Marx, who played upon this association to stigmatize capitalism itself, as "jewing" universalized. As we have seen in the previous essay, behind much of the Marxist critique of capitalism, indeed much of the socialist critique of capitalism, was the notion that commerce and finance were fundamentally unproductive.[79]

There were also nonsocialist variations of this theme, which maintained that farming, industry, and engineering are productive, but that commerce and finance are not. To late-nineteenth-century German anti-Semites, for example, Jews were *Luftmenschen*, "people of the air" who lacked a solid grounding in agriculture and industry. "Air" in this context was a symbol for trade and finance.[80] From their perspective, the Jews' economic profile was not only atypical, but pathological. This view was not confined to Europe. In the United States of the 1920s, Henry Ford published his series on "The International Jew" in his *Dearborn Inde-*

pendent, explaining that he was "only trying to awake the Gentile world to an understanding of what is going on. The Jew is a mere huckster, a trader who doesn't want to produce, but to make something out of what somebody else produces."[81]

Such notions associating trade with unproductivity found their echoes in Jewish circles as well. Some Jews came to accept, to a greater or lesser degree, the anti-Semitic critique of Jewish economic patterns. They internalized the connection that had long existed between anti-Semitism and anticapitalism. The Jewish campaign to move Jews from trade and commerce to more "productive" occupations had its antecedents in the Jewish enlightenment of the late eighteenth century. But it picked up steam a century later. From the late nineteenth century through the early decades of the twentieth, there were a series of attempts to move Jews from commerce and finance into crafts and agriculture.

One such response was found among German Jewish critics in the later nineteenth century, who regarded the Jews' concentration in commerce and professions as economically and psychically toxic.[82] German Jewish authors accused fellow Jews of being overly acquisitive and materialistic, of being "given over to Mammon."[83] In Vienna, officials of the Jewish community responded to anti-Semitic agitation by recommending that their members refrain from giving out loans at interest, and advised them to steer their children away from commerce and toward agricultural professions.[84] Much of labor Zionism was based upon the premise that Jews needed to distance themselves from trade and commerce, whether because physical labor was seen as ennobling (A. D. Gordon), or because of a belief that a productive national existence required the creation of a Jewish working class (Ber Borochov).[85]

In the twentieth century there were numerous non-Zionist attempts at planned, large-scale agricultural colonization. In the United States, the banker and philanthropist Jacob Schiff created the Jewish Immigrants Information Bureau in 1907 to encourage Jews to settle as farmers in Texas rather than crowd into New York as garment workers.[86] The largest Jewish colonization project of the interwar era, now hardly remembered, was the work of the Agro-Joint in the Soviet Union. From 1924 to 1938, it spent over 16 million dollars—most of it raised from wealthy American Jewish capitalists—to settle some 60,000 Jews on one million acres in the Ukraine and the Crimea. The plan failed dismally. It ran into ethnic opposition, first in Ukraine, then in Crimea. In the mid-1930s, Stalin's purges wiped out most of the Agro-Joint staff, and in 1941 the colonies themselves were destroyed by the Germans.[87] These were only the most salient of the many organized attempts by Jews to move Jews out of commerce.

In historical retrospect, these projects have a peculiar untimeliness: attempting to create Jewish farmers and industrial workers while capitalist development was moving toward an economy based on white-collar occupations, services, and the expansion of retailing. As we have seen, while would-be reformers of Jewry sought to move the Jews out of trade, Jews responded by moving themselves to where opportunities for trade were greater, namely out of Russia and eastern Europe and to the United States.

One place where this strategy made greater sense—that is, where it had a logic independent of the stigmatization of commerce as unproductive—was in the Zionist movement. To be sure, some Zionist thinkers, such as A. D. Gordon, were influenced by the romance of the peasantry as articulated by Leo Tolstoy, an ethos very much in evidence in the early kibbutz movement.[88] Others, especially Vladimir Jabotinksy, the founder of the Revisionist Zionist movement, rejected the socialist romanticization of the working class, valued the role of Jewish entrepreneurship, and sought to preserve it in a new Jewish state. Jabotinsky argued that the development of technology was leading to the declining significance of manual labor. Muscle and manual power were becoming ever less important, brain power more so. The future, Jabotinsky predicted, belonged not to the proletariat but to the bourgeoisie.[89] But, romanticism aside, the Zionist commitment to creating a new social structure was based on the assumption that a Jewish sovereign state, capable of self-defense, would require a society that included Jewish manual workers and farmers, as well as those engaged in more commercial, intellectual, or professional pursuits. The social theorist Ernest Gellner (to whom we return in the fourth chapter) captured the essence of the matter:

> Whether the kibbutzim do indeed provide the good life for modern man, as their founders believed and hoped, remains an open question; but as a piece of machinery for effectively re-settling the land by people drawn from heavily urbanized and embourgeoised populations, *and* effectively defending it in a military crisis with minimal and exiguous

means, they proved to be quite outstanding, and indeed unequalled.[90]

While the pre- and post-independence history of the state of Israel was ideologically stamped by socialist Zionism, the reality was more complex—and more capitalistic. The extent of private enterprise in the building of the *Yishuv* (the Jewish community in Palestine) and in the first decades of the state of Israel was more substantial than is commonly recognized, from the developers of citrus orchards to the creation of hydroelectric power in the years of the British mandate. And private Jewish capital from abroad, whether brought by new immigrants or invested by Jews living in the Diaspora, was an important factor in the state's economic development.[91] So was economic support provided by Jews in the Diaspora, who donated some of the money they had earned through capitalist enterprise to the fledgling Jewish state.

The economic history of the Jewish majority of the state of Israel was a speeded-up version of the economic history of Western capitalist societies. From a society with a large agrarian sector in its early years, it moved toward an industrial society and then to one in which services dominated.[92] Manual labor, always a minority taste, lost its mystique. After 1967, it was increasingly performed by Arabs from the occupied territories; and after the first Intifada, by foreign guestworkers.[93] As residents of a small country with limited population and natural resources, Israelis turned increasingly to international trade and investment. Having begun as a dirigiste economy, in which investment was controlled by the government or by banks and industrial conglomerates associated with the Labor and Religious (*Mizrachi*) parties, the country moved in the course of the 1980s toward the privatization of state-owned enterprises and the relaxation of government control of capital markets. By the 1990s, the country had become a center of entrepreneurial energy, with thousands of start-ups, and more companies traded on the major New York exchanges than any other country aside from the United States and Canada.[94] Thus, in Israel too, Jews have once again become a highly commercial nation, finding their historical proclivities well suited to the global economy.[95] Indeed, Israelis created their own diaspora, forming new transnational social networks that recapitulated the experiences of earlier Jewish diasporas.

Jacob Frankel and Stanley Fischer, leading economists formerly associated with the World

Bank and the International Monetary Fund, became governors of the Bank of Israel (the equivalent of the Federal Reserve Board in the United States). Fischer's life history exemplified the larger trajectory of Zionist attitudes toward capitalism. Born in Zambia in 1943, he grew up in what was then Southern Rhodesia, where he was active in the Labor Zionist youth movement, *Habonim*. After studies at the London School of Economics and MIT, he went on to become a professor of economics at MIT, where his doctoral students included Ben Bernanke. Fischer then became chief economist of the World Bank (where he was succeeded by Lawrence Summers), an officer of the IMF, and then vice chairman of Citigroup, before moving to Israel in 2005 to become governor of the Bank of Israel.

As we have seen then, Milton Friedman's contention that Jews vilified capitalism while profiting from it is highly distorted. To the extent that Jews identified themselves with socialism, it was largely a phenomenon of eastern European Jews and their immediate descendents in the years from the late nineteenth century through the 1930s. It is true that leading socialist intellectuals were of Jewish origin—but then, so were leading proponents of capitalism.

Because Jews are highly overrepresented in intellectual professions, they tended to be salient as ideological spokesmen of almost every political tendency, from the New Left to the New Right. By the time Friedman published his thoughts on Jews and capitalism in 1984, Jewish intellectuals and politicians were emerging as leading voices in favor of more market-oriented policies. In the United States there was not only Friedman himself, but his close intellectual associates such as Aaron Director, Gary Becker, and Richard Posner. Irving Kristol emerged as the godfather of neoconservatism and a leading intellectual defender of capitalism, while on the libertarian fringe there were the disciples of Ayn Rand (herself a Russian Jew), such as Alan Greenspan; and the disciples of Ludwig von Mises (like Rand, a nonidentifying Jew), who included Israel M. Kirzner, an economist and theorist of entrepreneurship who was also an Orthodox rabbi. In England, Margaret Thatcher's leading programmatic thinker was Keith Joseph; another was Leon Brittan, both of whom were Jewish. Thatcher presided over a cabinet that probably had a higher percentage of Jews than any government outside of Israel since the Hungarian Soviet Republic of 1919, including Nigel Lawson as Chancellor of the Exchequer. Jewish electorates throughout much of Europe had long moved away from parties of the Left,[96] and socialism was becoming a residual phenomenon in the state of Israel. In the United States, Jews tended to vote for the Democratic party, but it was "socialist" only in the eyes of those who regarded any departure from laissez-faire capitalism as socialist. Jews were salient both in the populist wing of the party that was most suspicious of the market (such as Paul Wellstone, the senator from Minnesota), and in the more market-oriented factions of the party, such as the Democratic Leadership Council, headed by Al From.

In accounting for Jewish antipathy to capitalism, Friedman pointed more plausibly to another motivation: "to demonstrate to themselves and the world the fallacy of the anti-Semitic stereotype"[97] of the Jew as greedy and materialistic, by showing generosity and public-spiritedness. Here, again, one suspects that he is on to something. But it is not the Jewish embrace of socialism. For generosity, not to speak of public spiritedness, has often been embraced by Jewish capitalists. Indeed Jewish capitalists have tended to play a disproportionate role in philanthropy, both in Europe and in the United States. The history of Jewish philanthropy—both toward Jewish causes and toward non-Jewish ones—is an intrinsic part of the Jewish response to capitalism.

Yet if Jews have been less enthusiastic about socialism than Friedman would have us believe, a suspicion of the moral and spiritual hazards presented by capitalism has been a recurrent motif of both Jewish religious preaching and of the Jewish novel. The life of selling was fraught with temptations to deceive or shade the truth; the rich were prone to self-glorification, at the expense of the pious and the learned; and affluence, when it came, was often seen as a snare, leading away from holiness and toward material excess. These are salient themes in two of the late masterworks of Yiddish literary realism—Isaac Bashevis Singer's *The Manor* and *The Estate* (1967–69) and Chaim Grade's *Tsemakh Atlas* (1967; published in English as *The Yeshiva*).[98]

The American Experience in Comparative Perspective

Because of the ongoing association of the Jews with commerce, both in Europe and in America, a fundamentally positive view of commerce within the larger society tended to lead to a favorable or at least neutral disposition toward the Jews. Here we find the greatest difference between continental European societies, on the one hand, and British and American society on the other. In Europe there were a number of traditions that were fundamentally suspicious of commerce, including Catholicism, the anticommercial ethos of many aristocracies, and the suspicion of merchants among peasants. From at least the eighteenth century on, there were continuous laments by conservatives about the destabilizing effects of trade on local tastes and mores. And then, of course, there was socialism, with its principled opposition to commerce, and all too often to the ethnic group most identified with commerce (though by and large socialist and Communist parties adopted a policy of opposition to anti-Semitism). Each of these traditions existed in the United States as well, but in a much weaker form. It is a cliché of American history that the founders and framers were deeply steeped in Lockean liberalism—but it is true. And that liberalism viewed private property and market activity as essential components of the pursuit of happiness. Thus the identification of Jews with market activity and commercial acumen, which so often worked against them in Europe, more frequently worked in their favor in the American context.[99]

Yet even in a fundamentally commercial society there is a propensity toward what Nietzsche called *ressentiment*—the hatred of the more accomplished by the less successful, and the attempt to rationalize failure by delegitimating achievement. Joseph Schumpeter regarded resentment as the almost inevitable byproduct of the dynamism that is characteristic of capitalism; and Friedrich Hayek noted that it was the Jews who were often made to bear the brunt of such resentment.[100] That resentment came not only from the lower classes, but from the members of the erstwhile upper classes when they found themselves losing their relative social status as new money displaced old. For old money, the makers of new money are by definition pushy and aggressive parvenus. This held for upper-class Americans as well (think of Henry Adams), though to a lesser extent than their German, Hungarian, or British counterparts. The Jews' relative success at capitalist activity—as merchants, financiers, and professionals—made them the objects of opprobrium. This resentment of the dynamic and the successful has haunted every merchant minority.[101] As Thomas Sowell has noted, the rapid rise of immigrant minorities creates new resentments among a variety of groups:

> While some observers might regard [their] determination and resourcefulness as admirable or inspiring, to others the rise of middleman minorities from poverty to prosperity has been like a slap across the face. If accepted as an achievement, it raises painful questions about others who have achieved nothing comparable, despite in some cases being initially more fortunate. Someone who was born rich represents no such assault on the ego and creates no such resentment or hostility. Anyone who can offer an alternative explanation of these middlemen's success—such as calling them "parasites" or "bloodsuckers" who have prospered at the expense of others—has been popular in many countries and some have built entire careers and whole movements on such popularity. When people are presented with the alternatives of hating themselves for their failure or hating others for their success, they seldom choose to hate themselves.[102]

In both Europe and America, perspicacious Jews, consciously or tacitly aware of the antipathy brought on by their success, have responded with two strategies. One is philanthropy, by conspicuous contribution to the culture and social welfare of the larger (non-Jewish) community.[103] A second strategy was to try to alleviate the pain of those who are less successful in capitalist societies, including through governmental income transfers. For those who regard any departure from free-market capitalism as "socialist," support for the welfare state is deemed anticapitalist. But it is eminently reconcilable with capitalism, and arguably the necessary complement that helps ensure the long-term survival of capitalist societies. However we judge the moral desirability of welfare-state income transfers, it should be clear that groups that combine economic success with the awareness that their success is an object of suspicion have a particular incentive to avoid circumstances in which the less successful challenge the very basis of economic success. This is not the only factor explaining the propensity of Jews to vote for the Democratic party, but it is an often neglected one. Cultural commitments also play a role: to the extent that the Republican party is perceived as defining American identity in Christian terms, it tends to repel Jews, just as Christianist parties in Europe once did. And for some Jews, especially those most distant from traditional Judaism, being "on the Left" has become an *ersatz* form of Jewish identity.

As was his wont, Milton Friedman raised issues that others were loathe to touch, from the possibility of school vouchers to the advantages of a negative income tax. His "Capitalism and the Jews" was an intellectual provocation, serving as a stimulus to historical reflection. There are, no doubt, individual Jews who perfectly embody Friedman's paradox—who act capitalistically while remaining fundamentally antipathetic to capitalism. Some may be simply hypocritical, or ideologically schizophrenic: but they are far from alone in compartmentalizing their minds into mutually exclusive spheres. But as we have seen, Friedman's claims about the economic success of the Jews under capitalism bear up better than his generalizations about their ideological response. The passage of time and new explorations by historians of modern Jewry allow for a more nuanced reconstruction of Jewish responses to capitalism. It turns out that those responses were more favorable than Friedman had imagined.

CHAPTER THREE

RADICAL ANTICAPITALISM
The Jew as Communist

It is among the remarkable facts of modern European history that Jews were identified by others not only with capitalism, but with the most extreme form of anticapitalism, namely Communism. If, as we have seen, anti-Semitism was often linked to anticapitalism, the existence of anti-Semitism helped to push some Jews toward a movement that promised to eliminate anti-Semitism by abolishing its purported roots in capitalism itself. But the identification of Jews with Communism actually served to bolster anti-Semitism. The result was a dialectic of disaster: anti-Semitism led Jews to prominent positions in Communist movements, and their very salience in a movement that threatened existing society provided new fuel for anti-Semitism.[1]

The myth of the Jew as Bolshevik emerged from the wave of revolutions at the close of World War I. The notion became central to the Nazi program of ideological anti-Semitism, and helped inspire the collaboration of non-Germans throughout eastern Europe in that program's murderous execution during World War II. After the war, the dialectic of anti-Semitism and Jewish involvement in Communism continued to influence the history of eastern Europe, as the conspicuous role played by men and women of Jewish origin in the Sovietization of eastern Europe once again transformed anti-Semitism, this time into an adjunct of popular opposition to Stalinism. And then, in a final twist, the Soviets and the Communists of eastern Europe endeavored to use this new anti-Semitism for their own ends.

The pernicious interaction of right-wing anti-Semitism and Jewish support for revolutionary Communism has not gone unnoticed, but few have appreciated its significance for the history of modern Jewry and of modern Europe. My purpose here is to sketch the contours of the tale, focusing not, as most scholars have done, on questions of motivation, but on consequences, intended and unintended. The case of Hungary will get particular attention because it so strikingly demonstrates the larger pattern. For in Hungary, many of the typical processes of modern Jewish history seemed to occur in a concentrated and exaggerated fashion. Nowhere, perhaps, was the economic and social ascent of Jews so rapid as in Hungary in the half-century before World War I. The position of Jews in Communist revolutions at the end of that war was nowhere more salient than in Hungary. The Holocaust came late to Hungarian Jewry, and occurred with a speed unrivaled elsewhere. After World War II, Hungary was again an extreme example of the representation of Jews in the new Communist government brought to power by the Red Army.

While the identification by anti-Semites of Jews with capitalism was based upon an exaggeration, the identification of Jews with Communism was based upon a distortion. The identification of Jews with capitalism was based on an exaggeration of the reality that Jews really tended to be more successful capitalists. The identification of Jews with Communism was grounded in the fact that while few Jews were in fact Communists, men and women of Jewish origin were particularly salient in Communist movements. "Judeo-Bolshevism" was a myth. But like many myths, it had just enough connection to reality to make it a plausible specter.

The universalism of Marxism, its promise to end all distinctions based upon ethnic or religious origin, to provide brotherhood with the gentiles, made it attractive to young Jews, as well as other ethnic minorities. Most often, it took the form of attraction to socialism, a movement with strong democratic roots, and one that transformed itself in the course of the twentieth century into a reformist force within capitalist society. But a sizable minority of young Jews (often, but not always of Russian Jewish origin) was attracted to the more radical and revolutionary movement of Communism. And this occurred in a remarkable range of settings: from Russia to the United States, from Egypt to South Africa.[2] It proved to be a fatal attraction.

In eastern and central Europe, especially, the link between Jews and Communism loomed large for much of the twentieth century. There Jewish experience was played out against a background of deeply ingrained anti-Semitic sentiment. In the Russian empire and in Romania, that sentiment was expressed on the official level by the denial of citizenship rights, by restrictions on residency, and by limited access to educational institutions, and on the popular level by pogroms. In the relatively more liberal empires of Germany and Austria-Hungary, anti-Semitism was more subtle and less onerous. But in both eastern and central Europe the nature of anti-Semitism—its intensity, focus, and vigor—was soon to be influenced and sometimes transformed by Jewish revolutionaries, whose actions would be interpreted through a filter of existing anti-Semitic prejudice and taken as representative of Jewry as a whole.

Any such exploration faces the dilemma of defining who is to be considered a Jew. Is the historian to include those who deliberately and explicitly dissociated themselves from Judaism and Jewry (such as Karl Marx, converted by his apostate father to Lutheranism at the age of four)? To regard such people as Jewish might appear to accept the racist categories imposed upon Jews by their enemies. Were one to accept solely the definitions of anti-Semites, one might end up counting even those with no historical link to Jewry, such as Joseph Stalin, whose real surname of Dzhugashvili, according to an expatriate Ukrainian anti-Semite, is Georgian for "son of a Jew." In considering the historical relationship of Jews, Communism, and anti-Semitism, it would seem most useful to regard as Jews those who were so regarded by others and who were actually of Jewish origin. Much of the attraction of Communism lay in the desire to *escape* that origin, which was identified with particularism, parochialism, backwardness, and often enough, with commerce.[3]

The Soviet Crucible

An article in the London *Illustrated Sunday Herald* from February 1920, entitled "Zionism versus Bolshevism—A Struggle for the Soul of the Jewish People," describes Bolshevism as "the schemes of International Jews. . . . Now at last this band of extraordinary personalities from the underworld of the great cities of Europe and America have gripped the Russian people by the hair of their heads, and have become practically the undisputed masters of that enormous empire."

The author of this article, Winston Churchill, was expressing a view shared by many opponents of Bolshevism in Russia and abroad, to whom the prominence of men of Jewish origin in the Bolshevik leadership was unmistakable.[4] Leon Trotsky, commissar for foreign affairs in Lenin's first cabinet, had organized the coup within the Petrograd Soviet in 1917 that set off the October Revolution and overthrew the liberal government of Alexander Kerensky. Other prominent Bolsheviks of Jewish origin included the president of the Supreme Soviet, Yakov Sverdlov; the deputy chairman of the Council of Peoples' Commissars and chairman of the Moscow Soviet, Lev Kamenev (born Rosenfeld); the president of the Petrograd Soviet and leader of the Communist International, Grigori Zinoviev (born Radomyslski); the head of the Petrograd Cheka (secret police), Moisei Uritsky; and Karl Radek (born Sobelsohn), who was a leading figure in the Russian and German Communist parties.

With so many Bolsheviks of Jewish origin in positions of leadership, it was easy to consider Bolshevism a "Jewish" phenomenon. And if Winston Churchill, who was personally remote from anti-Semitism, could regard Bolshevism as a disease of the Jewish body politic, those who had long conceived of Jews as the enemies of Christian civilization quickly concluded that Bolshevism was little more than a transmutation of the essence of the Jewish soul. By almost any logic, however, the identification of Bolshevism with the Jews was mistaken. To be sure, most Russian Jews welcomed the fall of the czarist regime, which had abetted anti-Semitism, confined most Jews to the "Pale of Settlement," and radically restricted their access to higher education. Within living memory, the czarist government had expelled the Jews from Moscow (1891); tolerated and even encouraged pogroms against hundreds of Jewish settlements in the wake of the revolutions of 1905; tried Mendel Beilis in 1911 on the charge of murdering a gentile boy to use his blood for Jewish ritual purposes; and, after blaming the defeats of the Russian army in 1914 on the Jews, deported hundreds of thousands of them to the Russian interior.

But after the revolution of February 1917, Jewish legal disabilities were ended by the Kerensky government. Moreover, governmental anti-Semitism, despite its severity, had not driven most Jews to the radical Left. In czarist Russia, most politically active Jews were not socialists. In the first Russian Duma of 1906, there were twelve Jews, nine of whom were associated with the liberal Constitutional Democrats. Of those Jews who were socialists, most identified with the Yiddishist *Bund*, a smaller number with the Zionist *Poalei Zion*, a smaller number yet with the Mensheviks, and the tiniest minority with the Bolsheviks. The reason most Russian Jews did not support Bolshevism in 1917 was that its atheism contradicted Jewish religious belief, and its economic policy threatened the many Jewish merchants, traders, and shopkeepers. In 1918 the rabbis of Odessa anathematized the Jewish Bolsheviks. The chief rabbi of Moscow, Jacob Mazeh, is said to have told Trotsky (born Bronstein), "The Trotskys make the revolutions, and the Bronsteins pay for it." This was a theme voiced time and again as the official Jewish community beheld with apprehension the prominence of Jews in the revolutionary wave.

Only once the civil war was under way did Jews begin to swing toward the Bolsheviks, and then not out of intrinsic attraction to the Reds but rather out of an instinct of self-preservation against the massive pogroms that accompanied the fighting. In 1919, the Red Army, with Trotsky at its head, moved into the Ukraine; the Ukrainian nationalist commander Hryhoriiv, in his appeal for help against the Bolsheviks, claimed that "the people who crucified Christ rule the Ukraine," while other partisan bands adopted the slogan "Death to Jews! For the Orthodox faith."

In fact, in the confused circumstances in Byelorussia and the Ukraine, murderous attacks on Jews were a matter less of high policy than of popular peasant sentiment. The directory of the Ukrainian National Republic and the White leader, Denikin, tried in vain to control local commanders for whom the breakdown of order afforded an opportunity to plunder and murder. As the battle turned, some of these commanders switched sides, and continued their pogroms under Bolshevik auspices. Some 70,000 Jews were murdered in the Ukraine, and another 50,000 by the Whites of Denikin's Russian Volunteer Army. The effect was to drive Jews into the arms of the Reds; they had concluded that for better or worse, their very lives now depended on the defeat of the counterrevolution.

In the years following, the pattern of Jewish engagement with Bolshevism became dangerously skewed. Jews were somewhat overrepresented in the Bolshevik party, as were other ethnic groups that had suffered from discrimination. But since Jews were more highly urbanized and more highly educated than the other groups, they were more likely to be activists, and once within the party, were more likely to rise. From 1917 to 1922, between one-sixth and one-fifth of the delegates to the Bolshevik party congresses were of Jewish origin. In the 1920s Jews comprised about 5 percent of the membership of the Communist party of the USSR, or about twice their proportion in the population.

Since most of the prerevolutionary civil service and intelligentsia refused to collaborate with the Bolsheviks or remained suspect in Bolshevik eyes, educated Jews moved into important and especially sensitive positions in the bureaucracy and administration of the new regime. As a result, for many Russians, their first encounter with the new regime was likely to be with a commissar, tax officer, or secret-police official of Jewish origin. To these people, the sociology of the Communist movement was a matter of little interest. Their anti-Semitism confirmed, they now conflated the Jew-as-commissar with their age-old image of the Jew-as-deicide.

The rapid movement of Jews into the economic, cultural, and political fields continued through the 1920s and reached its high point in the mid-1930s.[5] In 1926, the last Jewish member was appointed to the Politburo: he was Lazar Kaganovich, who later presided over the politically motivated famine in the Ukraine that took the lives of millions of Ukrainian peasants. The multilinguality of the Communists of Jewish origin also led to their overrepresentation in the Comintern, and their key role in organizing new Communist movements around the world.[6] During the Great Purge of 1934–39, Jews were overrepresented among the purgers (as employees of the secret police) and among the purged. They included Genrikh Yagoda, who served as head of the secret police from 1934 until he himself was purged in 1936.[7] But for every purged Jewish Communist such as Yagoda, there were far more Jewish victims drawn from the ranks of the religious, the Zionists, and others at fundamental odds with the regime. As the purges replaced existing functionaries with those of peasant and blue-collar origin, the representation of Jews in the party and state apparatus fell precipitously.[8] Just before the outbreak of World War II, a campaign to cleanse the Soviet elite of ethnic Jews was launched, which picked up steam after 1948 and reached fever pitch in the "Doctors' Plot," shortly before Stalin's death in 1953.[9]

Aborted Revolutions in Germany

In central Europe, and especially in Germany, the story differed somewhat.[10] By 1918, most German Jews had already moved into the middle and even upper classes, and so there was no goad of poverty driving them toward socialism. On the contrary, in their voting and in their political activism, German Jews, largely reflecting their social and economic status as members of the middle class, identified as far to the right as the political spectrum allowed. That, however, was not very far. As in most of Europe, the doors to the political Right were slammed in Jewish faces by parties that regarded Christianity as integral to national identity. (In Italy, where the Right was least prone to anti-Semitism, bourgeois Jews joined the

Fascist party and some rose to positions of prominence.)

And so most German Jews voted for the liberals in the decades before World War I. However, most political *activists* of Jewish origin were to be found in the ranks of the socialists. Some of them were led to the socialist camp by their quest for greater political and social equality. For while German Jews had already been guaranteed their civil and political rights, as they moved up the social and educational ladder, they often found their path to governmental posts blocked and their opportunities for academic advance limited not by law but by prejudice. But other Jews were drawn to a more apocalyptic conception of socialist revolution.

The high culture of the educated classes of western and central Europe in the decade before 1914 was marked by a disaffection from liberal, bourgeois "society" and a search for new sources of "community." In time, this disaffection would lead many young German intellectuals to the radical Right, to a new nationalism that promised a sense of collective purpose based on a purportedly shared past. For those Jewish intellectuals steeped in the antiliberal ethos but by definition excluded from movements seeking a return to Germanic roots, the alternatives were a turn to Zionism (which only a few embraced before 1918) or toward a visionary socialism that promised to replace the supposedly atomizing civilization of liberal capitalism with a new culture of shared purpose that would unite all men regardless of origin.

With the collapse of the German monarchy in November 1918, Jews moved into positions of government responsibility and saliency for the first time. Like their non-Jewish counterparts, most Jewish socialists in Germany welcomed the breakthrough to full parliamentary democracy produced by the mass demonstrations of the working class at the close of the war. Real power was temporarily shared between a provisional government made up of parliamentary representatives of the socialist and liberal parties, on the one hand, and the councils of workers and soldiers on the other. The Left thus confronted a political choice. The Social Democrats favored parliamentary sovereignty, to be decided by democratic elections among the entire populace. To their left were the Spartacists, who formed the new Communist party, devoted to the sovereignty of the councils (the German equivalent of the soviets). Between them were the Independent

Socialists, who vacillated on the question of parliamentary versus council control.

In the fateful months after 1918, the parliamentary democratic aspirations of the Social Democrats were challenged by a series of revolutions in Berlin and Munich. Ultimately the Social Democratic leaders chose to call upon elements of the old imperial army and the newly formed Free Corps to combat the threat from the radical Left. The decision was ominous, for young veterans of the counterrevolutionary corps later became the backbone of National Socialism. That the leaders of the suppressed revolutions were so often Jews was a crucial factor in the recrudescence of political anti-Semitism in Germany.

The involvement of Jews in the new Communist party of Germany displayed the same inverted pyramid pattern found elsewhere.[11] Among the Jewish population as a whole, support for the Communists was insignificant. Jews were somewhat overrepresented, however, among party activists, comprising about 7 percent of the participants at the party's founding convention. As for the eleven-person central committee, it included four Communists of Jewish origin: Rosa Luxemburg, Leo Jogiches, Paul Levi, and August Thalheimer, all of them university-educated.

Born in Poland and long active as a theorist and agitator in the Polish and German socialist movements, Rosa Luxemburg had spurned parliamentary democracy as a "petty-bourgeois illusion" and referred to the German Social Democrats as the *Schabbesgoyim* (gentiles engaged to perform work not permitted to religious Jews on the Sabbath) of the German capitalists. The theorist of "revolutionary spontaneity," Luxemburg had long spurred the German proletariat to revolutionary action. In her editorials for the party newspaper, *The Red Flag*, she wrote in December 1918, "In this, the ultimate class struggle of world history and for the sake of the highest goals of humanity, the slogan in regard to our enemies must be 'Thumbs in their eyes, knees to their chest.'" So when the leadership of the Communists called for an armed rising in January 1919, Luxemburg felt duty-bound to support it, even though it enjoyed little popular backing. She was brutally murdered by soldiers of the Free Corps whom the Social Democratic government had called in to suppress the revolt.

In Bavaria, the apex of the revolutionary turmoil was occupied by a coterie of Jewish intellectuals almost totally lacking in political experience. The revolution in Bavaria was planned and headed by Kurt Eisner of the Independent

Socialists, who on November 7, 1918, declared the end of the monarchy and the rise of a Bavarian republic. The Munich working classes were swept by a wave of revulsion against the monarchy, which had led the country into the war. It was this disgust with the old regime that allowed Eisner, a bearded, bohemian Jewish theater critic, to come to power in conservative, Catholic, rural, anti-Semitic Bavaria. When the Jewish citizens of Munich wrote begging Eisner to resign in favor of a non-Jew, he responded that the question of origins belonged to "an age that has now been overcome," and remained at the helm.

Massive unemployment and food shortages soon became the order of the day in the new Bavarian Republic, which faced staggering problems of demobilization and the threat of government insolvency due to unrealistic new social welfare policies. Eisner was a man of high ideals but poor judgment, whose rhetorical radicalism and tactical inconsistency managed to alienate almost all political factions. In January 1919 his party received 2.5 percent of the vote; while on his way to tender his resignation, he was assassinated by a young aristocrat.

After a confused transitional period, a new government, made up in good part of leftist intellectuals of Jewish origin, came to power in

Munich on April 7, and declared a Soviet republic. The short-lived regime included the an-
archist Gustav Landauer; the playwright Ernst
Toller, who announced that the coming of socialism would mean "the liberation of man
from all capitalist and spiritual oppression";
the radical orator Erich Mühsam, whose politics were characterized by a friend as the constant attempt to stand to the left of himself;
and Otto Neurath, a socialist theorist who became commissar for socialization. His plans for
socialization of almost everything did not get
beyond the stage of proclamations, but he was
in office long enough to terrify the Bavarian
middle and upper classes. After a week, the first
Bavarian Socialist Republic was replaced by a
more radical group affiliated with the Communist International, which proclaimed the Second Bavarian Soviet Republic. It was headed by
Eugen Leviné-Nissen, a Russian-born follower
of Rosa Luxemburg who had been dispatched
to Munich by the Communist party. The Social Democrats, the largest party in the elected
Bavarian parliament, looked to Berlin for help
in repressing the Communists. Troops were
duly dispatched by the central government and
joined by Free Corps from northern Bavaria.
They marched into Munich in May, overturn-

ing the Bavarian Soviet Republic in a wave of terror.

Among those who lived through the trauma of the soviet republics was the recently demobilized Adolf Hitler. His anti-Semitism predated the trauma, but it was in its aftermath that he hit upon one of his most seductive themes: the "Jewish-Marxist world conspiracy."

Most German Jews felt no enthusiasm for the events of November 1918, which they, like many of their fellow Germans, regarded as a national disaster. Moreover, Jewish newspapers in Munich and elsewhere warned that the prominence of revolutionary Jews would lead to increased anti-Semitism. In this, they were correct. When Kurt Eisner was murdered in February 1919, the *Kreuzzeitung*, the venerable organ of Prussian conservatism, opined that he "was among the most evil representatives of the Jews, who in recent months have played so marked a role in German history. In the most prominent way, he combined two characteristics of his race, its historical internationalism— for Eisner too is a foreigner by birth [*sic*]—and its racially based idle fancy, in contrast to German realism." Here, then, was another element in the emerging dialectic of disaster: the new image of the Jew implanted in the mind of the

German public was derived from the activities of those Jews who were most removed from Judaism or a concern with the fate of Jewry.

The anti-Semites of the German Right did not, of course, restrict their hatred to the Jewish advocates of a Soviet Germany. Their antipathy extended to social democrats and liberal democrats as well. But it was the chance to associate social democrats and liberals with Jewish Communists that made the image of the Jewish Communist revolutionary so useful to the German Right. A Nationalist party poster of 1919 listed, under the heading "Varieties of Cohens," the Communist, Social Democratic, Independent Socialist, and Democratic parties alongside portraits of leading Jewish politicians in each party.

Hungary

If Jews were highly visible in the revolutions in Russia and Germany, in Hungary they seemed omnipresent.[12]

Virtually forgotten today but widely resonant in its time was the Hungarian Soviet Republic. It began with the collapse of the liberal government in March 1919 and lasted for 133 days until, weakened by inner disintegration, it succumbed to foreign troops. Of the government's forty-nine commissars, thirty-one were of Jewish origin. Among the key members of the Hungarian Soviet Republic were Béla Kun, the foreign secretary and actual head of the regime; Tibor Szamuely, the deputy commissar for war, charged with suppressing the counter-revolution; and Ottó Korvin (Klein), the chief of the secret police. Others included Georg Lukács, the aesthetic philosopher turned Bolshevik, and Mátyás Rákosi (Roth), who three decades later was to become dictator of Hungary. As chairman of the revolutionary governing council they elected Sándor Garbai, a gentile. Rákosi later joked that Garbai was chosen for his post in order "to have someone who could sign the death sentences on Saturday."

The prominence of Jews in the Hungarian Soviet Republic is all the more striking when one considers that the Jews of Hungary were richer than their coreligionists in eastern Europe and remarkably successful in attaining positions of status. In the nineteenthth century, Jews had been the major agents of capitalist development in a traditional, rural society comprised of aristocrats, gentry, and peasantry. In the latter part of the century, the children of these Jewish entrepreneurs often entered the universities and moved into the professions.

Though only 5 percent of the population, on the eve of World War I Jews made up almost half the doctors, lawyers, and journalists in Hungary. Unlike their counterparts elsewhere, the Magyar upper classes welcomed Jewish assimilation into Hungarian culture, since this added weight to claims of Magyar hegemony in the ethnic balance within the Hungarian half of the Austro-Hungarian empire. Accomplished Jews intermarried with the nobility, were themselves ennobled, and attained positions of high prestige. On the eve of the war the government of Hungary included six or eight ministers of Jewish origin.

The term *of Jewish origin* is especially important in the case of Hungary. For peculiar historical reasons, access to the higher ranks of society and government was largely conditional upon conversion to Christianity. Thus the agnostic, secularized, educated children of the Jewish bourgeoisie were confronted with the bizarre fact that their entry into the rather liberal, even anticlerical Hungarian establishment required that they undergo the ritual of baptism. Some declined the offer as a hypocritical farce. Others decided that Budapest was worth a mass, only to find themselves confronted by an acute crisis of identity. In either case, the secularized Jewish intelligentsia of Hungary was naturally attracted to the ideology of radical internationalist socialism, which promised a political community based on universalism rather than on religious or national particularism. The literature of prerevolutionary Hungarian radicalism is rife with attacks on Judaism and the Jews—attacks often penned by intellectuals of Jewish origin.

When they seized power in 1919 the revolutionaries acted in accordance with their principles. Statues of Hungarian kings and national heroes were torn down, the national anthem was banned, and the display of the national colors was made a punishable offense. Nor did the revolutionaries forget their antipathy to *Jewish* particularism: traditionalist Jews became the targets of their campaigns of terror.

Radical agitators were dispatched to the countryside, where they ridiculed the institution of the family and threatened to turn churches into movie theaters. Their economic policy reflected the disdain that, as Marxists, they felt toward markets, moneymaking, and private property. More thoroughgoing than Lenin, the Hungarian revolutionaries socialized all estates over one hundred acres in size, rather than distributing land to the peasants. Nationalized too were business establishments with over ten employees, all apartments, all furniture "superfluous for everyday life," gold, jewelry, and coin and stamp collections. The principles of egalitarianism were strenuously applied. All wages were made uniform. All graves in Budapest were to be identical, and the sale of double plots forbidden. Much of the bourgeois press was first censored, then closed down.

The regime's policies soon alienated most Hungarians. Uniform wages combined with a government guarantee of employment led to a radical decline of productivity. The regime attempted to set all prices, with little regard to production costs. Goods were soon scarce and prices on the black market were highly inflated. Peasants chose to withhold agricultural goods, rather than exchange them for currency with which they could buy little.

Antipathy soon enough focused on the Jews. Young revolutionary intellectuals of Jewish origin had been sent to the countryside to administer the newly collectivized agricultural estates; their radicalism was exceeded only by their incompetence, reinforcing peasant anti-Semitism. The Jesuits, for their part, interpreted the revolution as Jewish and anti-Christian in essence, though the regime's antireligious campaign was in fact headed by a defrocked priest. Rumors abounded that the revolutionaries were everywhere desecrating the Host. In Budapest as in the countryside, opposition to the regime, defense of the church, and anti-Semitism went hand in hand.

The Kun regime fell in 1919, overwhelmed by political and economic difficulties and ultimately crushed by Romanian troops acting with the encouragement of Hungarian opponents of the regime. When the Romanians withdrew from Budapest, they turned over power to Admiral Horthy and the Magyar ruling class. After the Red terror—some 600 executions in 133 days in a country of eight million—came the White terror of the counterrevolution, aimed not only at officials and sympathizers of the fallen Red regime but at the Jewish community as such.

The Magyar ruling class, which before the war would not have tolerated such behavior, accepted the excesses as a necessary reaction to the terror that had preceded it. Though the situation of the Jews improved in the 1920s under the rather liberal regime of Count Bethlen, the Hungarian ruling class came under ever greater pressure from the radical Right, which had been forged in the counterrevolution and had made political anti-Semitism the core of its program.

The Myth of the Jew as Bolshevik

Political anti-Semitism as a distinct movement was itself a recent development on the European scene. Until the nineteenth century, European anti-Semitism had been predominantly religious in nature, grounded in the antipathy of the Christian churches to those who willingly spurned the ideas of the gospels. But with the development of industrial capitalism in the nineteenth century, the focus changed: it was now the Jew as capitalist who was attacked as the destroyer and despoiler of traditional society. For the new political anti-Semites, the Rothschilds and Bleichröders were *rois de l'époque*, the kings of the age. In western and central Europe, anti-Semitism of this stripe reached its height in the last decades of the nineteenth century, and seemed on the wane by 1914. But the conspicuous role of Jews in the revolutions of 1917–19 gave anti-Semitism a new impetus. Now the Jew as revolutionary took his place alongside the Jew as deicide and the Jew as capitalist; the images of Trotsky, Luxemburg, and Kun were superimposed upon those of Rothschild and Ahasuerus, the wandering Jew of medieval Christian myth, rootless and eternally cursed for having spurned Christ.

Among the books that spread the image

of the Jew as Communist revolutionary was *Quand Israël est roi* ("When Israel Is King"), an eyewitness account of the Hungarian Soviet Republic published in 1921 by Jean and Jérôme Tharaud. The authors, long identified with the French radical Right, were former winners of the Prix Goncourt and well known for a series of travel books merging reportage with poetic evocation. Their new book portrayed the Hungarian revolution as a Jewish conspiracy, with some non-Jews thrown in as figureheads. "After the dynasty of the Arpid, after St. Stephen and his sons, after the Anjous and the Hunyadis and the Hapsburgs, there was a King of Israel in Hungary today," the brothers reported, and went on to describe in lurid and somewhat fanciful detail the terror of the "Lenin Boys" (the Red Guard) and the torture employed by the political-investigation department under Ottó Korvin. Interspersed with accounts of the confiscation of wealth by the revolutionaries and the replacement of Christian professors by young Jewish intellectuals were reflections such as this: "A New Jerusalem was growing up on the banks of the Danube. It emanated from Karl Marx's Jewish brain, and was built by Jews upon a foundation of very ancient ideas." The book sold 55,000 copies in France, went through scores of editions, and was translated into other languages, including English and German. (In 1933 the Tharauds would entitle their book on the new Nazi regime *Quand Israël n'est plus roi*—"When Israel Is No Longer King.")

The image of the Jew as Bolshevik became the center of the new mythos of the Right. In its most radical and racist form, this mythos was read backward into history, as in the title of a pamphlet published in 1923 by Hitler's intellectual mentor, Dietrich Eckart, *Bolshevism from Moses to Lenin: A Dialogue between Adolf Hitler and Myself.* During the great German inflation of 1923, the Nazi party took banknotes made worthless by inflation and imprinted them with caricatured images of international Jewish Bolsheviks, such as Karl Radek and Alexander Helphand, described as *Ostjude Parvus-Helphand: Rumänischer Getreide Schieber. Geldgeber der Novemberverbrecher* (Eastern Jew Parvus-Helphand: Romanian grain profiteer. Funder of the November criminals).[13]

A clear-eyed analyst would have concluded that few Jews were, in fact, Communists, and that most Communists were not Jews. But Jewish Communists were viewed through a lens colored by previous anti-Semitic stereotypes. To conclude that the Jewish revolutionary and the Jewish capitalist were actually partners working both sides of the street on their road to the conquest of Christian civilization may have required a skewed vision, but this in fact was how the interwar Right viewed the Jewish question.

In the collective memory of American Jewry, the entanglement of Jews and Communism merits hardly a footnote. The handful who give much thought to the issue are more likely to regard the involvement of Jews with American Communism as a minor detour from the highway of integration into American democracy: a dead end perhaps, but in any case not an avenue of great consequence in the history of the United States or of American Jewry. After all, the party never came to power in the United States, not in a single state, not even in a single city. Yet the image of the Jew as Communist played an often overlooked role in the history not only of Jews in America, but of the millions of Jews in eastern Europe who would have liked to emigrate to the United States after World War I, but who were prevented from doing so by the immigration restrictions enacted in the early 1920s, culminating in the Reed-Johnson Act of 1924. For those restrictions were motivated in part by the identification of Jews with political radicalism. The notion of "Jewish Bolshevism" was a commonplace among American anti-Semites in the interwar years and beyond.[14]

Western and Eastern Europe

As for the depth, extent, and nature of anti-Semitism in the various European countries, that depended in large measure upon the economic, political, and cultural roles of the Jews in general, and not least upon the relative significance of the Jewish Communists. Where there had been no attempted revolutions, or where Jews played no conspicuous role in them, the myth of Jewish Bolshevism did not become predominant on the Right. This was the case in western Europe, which was spared both the revolutionary wave and the threat of Soviet conquest. (Although Italy did experience revolutionary seizures of land and industrial property in 1920 and 1921, few of the leaders of the radical Left had been Jews. In Italy, where the nationalist Right had long been open to those of Jewish origin, Jews were more likely to be found among the supporters of the Fascists than among the revolutionaries of the Left.)

By contrast, the identification of Jews with Communism was especially potent in those areas that had encountered Jewish revolutionaries firsthand in the postwar era: in Germany, Hungary, Poland, the Ukraine, and later Lithuania.[15]

We have already looked at the cases of Germany and Hungary. In Poland, the image of the Jew as Bolshevik was exacerbated by the fact that during the Soviet attack on the country in 1919, the Russians had set up a four-man Provisional Revolutionary Committee, two members of which were Jewish. Later, when eastern Poland and then Lithuania was annexed by the Soviet Union at the beginning of World War II, the Soviets, following a pattern that they were to repeat throughout eastern Europe, looked to the small and disproportionately Jewish band of Communists to assist them in establishing Soviet hegemony.

In no nation of eastern Europe did the Communist party have a broad popular base. (The Czech regions of Czechoslovakia were a partial exception.) This meant that even if a tiny proportion of Jews was attracted to Communism, the party would appear "Jewish." From among the 3.3 million Jews in interwar Poland, the Communist party garnered 5,000 members, but since the party's membership totaled only

20,000, this minuscule number of Jews made up a quarter of its membership. In Lithuania, one-third of the Communist party was made up of Jews in 1940—but there were only 2,000 Lithuanian Communists in all. Out of a Jewish population of 150,000, fewer than 700 were Communists, but in such cases it did not take very many Jewish Communists to make the party appear "Jewish" to outsiders. Similarly, in Romania, where 800,000 Jews lived at the beginning of World War II, the Romanian Communist party had a membership of less than a thousand, and a few thousand sympathizers, so that even if every party member was of Jewish origin (which was hardly the case), it would have amounted to an infinitesimal fraction of Romanian Jewry. But many posts in the upper echelons of the tiny party were filled by Jews, including Anna Pauker, the granddaughter of a rabbi.[16]

To be sure, in much of eastern Europe anti-Semitism long antedated the Bolshevik Revolution, and would have been a substantial factor in interwar politics even without the prominence of Jews in the Communist movement. In the new nations that emerged from the disintegration of the old Romanov and Habsburg empires, Jews were suspect for having identified with German, Russian, or Hungarian culture, rather than that of the new nationalities. In Hungary, Poland, and Romania, where Jews had long formed the bulk of the commercial and professional middle classes, their role was now challenged by the newly emerging gentile middle classes, whose opportunities for advancement were limited by the relatively constricted economy of the region. For these new aspiring middle classes, it was economically rewarding to regard the Jews as "outsiders." At the same time, Jews active in the commercialization of the rural economy were often resented by the peasantry, who blamed the Jews for their economic woes. The hatred of the Jew as Communist was thus one more ingredient in the anti-Semitic stew, in which the Jew might also be reviled as the representative of international capitalism, or as an ethnically foreign parasite on the body of the indigenous *Volk*, or as a competitor of the aspiring indigenous middle class.

In Germany, where political anti-Semitism had been on the wane before 1914, the role of Jews in the postwar revolutions was the key element in the revival of anti-Semitism on the Right. With Hitler's consolidation of his control over Germany, a coterie of ideologically radical anti-Semites stood at the head of the most powerful nation in Europe. After the

German invasion of the Soviet Union, this new anti-Semitism, fused with the pseudoscientific ideology of racism, guided the actions of Hitler's army and the SS. It soon developed into a campaign of extermination, a campaign in which the Germans were aided by indigenous accomplices throughout eastern Europe. The Nazis and their collaborators managed within a few years to murder six out of every seven Jews in eastern and central Europe.

After World War II

Yet in the years after Hitler's defeat, Jews appeared once again on the stage of East European politics. With the conquest of much of eastern and central Europe by the Red Army in 1944 and 1945, the dialectic of disaster took a new turn. Anti-Semitism led Jews to prominent positions in the sovietization of eastern Europe, as it had in the early stages of the Bolshevist regime. The process of their extrusion, which took decades in the Soviet Union, was compressed in eastern Europe.[17]

At the close of the war there were some 700,000 Jews in eastern Europe.[18] Some had managed to hide, others to survive the concentration camps. Hundreds of thousands of Jewish refugees from the region of Poland occupied by the Germans in 1939 had fled to the Soviet zone, whence they were deported by the Russians deep into the Soviet Union. Later, they were joined by Jewish refugees from eastern Poland, conquered by the Germans in 1941.

Those who survived the years in Siberia or the *kolkhozy* of central Asia returned to Poland after the war. Their firsthand experience of Communism in the USSR made them among the most eager to leave Soviet-occupied Poland for Palestine or the West. For the rest of the Jews of eastern and central Europe, however, the march of the Red Army literally saved their lives, and many welcomed the Russians with open arms. When they returned to their homes, the survivors often found them occupied by strangers. Their businesses, furniture, and even clothing had been claimed by others, who were appalled to witness the unanticipated return of these Jewish survivors, and engaged in threats and violence to keep them from reclaiming their property. This new confiscatory middle class had its own reasons for wanting to see the Jews vanish again, and played a role in the wave of pogroms that swept over eastern Europe in 1945 and 1946, the best known of which took place in Kielce in July 1946 at a cost of forty-one Jewish lives.

Yet these outbursts had another cause as well. Among the leading agents of Soviet control in Poland, Hungary, Romania, and Czechoslovakia were a handful of veteran Communists who had spent years in the Soviet Union while their parties had been outlawed and their homelands suffered under German occupation. Some of those who had returned with the Red Army were survivors of the Great Purge, their survival presumptive evidence of their loyalty to Stalin.

Many of the returning Communists—subsequently known as "Muscovites"—were Jews. In Hungary, as we shall see in greater detail below, the top leaders of the Communist party were Jewish Muscovites. In Czechoslovakia, the general secretary of the Communist party, Rudolf Slansky, was a Jew. Among the Muscovite Jewish leaders of postwar Poland were Jakub Berman, who headed the secret police; Hilary Minc, who was in charge of the economy; Roman Zambrowski (born Rubin Nussbaum), the secretary of the party's central committee; and Jacek Rozanski (born Goldberg), trained by the NKVD (the Soviet secret police), who became head of the investigative department of the ministry of public security. In Romania, the real head of the regime was Ana Pauker, secretary of the party central committee, first deputy prime minister, and foreign minister. Other pillars of the Romanian regime included Iosif Chisinevski, Leonte Rautu, and Mihail Roller—all Jewish Muscovites.

There were few Jewish Muscovites in the leadership of the East German regime, but this was because many of the German Jewish Communist exiles in the USSR who had managed to survive the Great Purge were handed over to the Gestapo in 1939 after the Molotov-Ribbentrop pact. One exception was Markus Wolf, the son of a Jewish Communist doctor from Stuttgart, who had spent his adolescence and young adulthood in Moscow and returned to Germany as an officer of the Red Army. Active at first in the propaganda apparatus of the regime, Wolf later built the East German military espionage service, which he headed until 1987. In addition to Wolf, there was also a small but significant trickle of Communist-oriented intellectuals of Jewish origin who had spent the war years in the West, and now returned to help create a Communist regime in Germany that would do away with what they regarded as the capitalist roots of National Socialism. Among the most conspicuous was Gerhard Eisler, a veteran functionary of the Comintern who vanished from the United States after he was subpoenaed by the House Committee on Un-American Activities in 1949. Eisler emerged in East Germany as the head of the new Office of Information, the propaganda ministry of the new regime. His brother Hanns Eisler left the United States under "voluntary deportation" in 1948, moved to East Germany, and wrote the music for the national anthem of the new German Democratic Republic.

The utilization of Jews in prominent positions in the Soviet-sponsored regimes was, to use an apposite phrase, "no accident." In the newly conquered nations of eastern and central Europe, the Soviets had few reliable supporters. Suspicion of Russian imperialism was old and well-founded, and anti-Communism almost a national religion. The tiny native Communist parties had been decimated during the war. The Muscovite Jews, tried and tested in the Stalinist crucible, were among the very few natives whom the Soviets could trust to carry out their plans. Some took on public leadership roles with reluctance, believing, as did Ana Pauker for example, that their ethnic origins would tend to discredit the party in the eyes of the anti-Semitic public.[19]

These veteran Communists were joined by younger Jews, disillusioned with the failed bourgeois assimilationism of their parents, having little knowledge of the Soviet Union, and attracted to an ideology that promised to do away with ethnic hatreds once and for all. Because they were familiar with local conditions and fanatically antifascist, Jews were often chosen for the security police. Because of their high level of education, they were particularly active in the fields of propaganda and education. Those who spoke foreign languages staffed the ministries of foreign affairs and departments of foreign trade. Thus, members of a people who had recently been deported or murdered amid the general indifference or active complicity of their neighbors now appeared as high officials of the government and the police. They did so under the auspices of the Red Army, and as the executors of the will of the Soviet Union. To much of the population of Poland, Romania, Hungary, and Czechoslovakia, these Jewish Communists appeared as aliens, imposing an alien system in the service of an alien power.

The upshot was a renewal of anti-Semitism. The local populace took no notice of the fact that the new Soviet-backed regimes subverted and then liquidated Jewish communal and religious institutions, or of the fact that most local Jews, far from supporting the Communists, voted with their feet by emigrating westward. Hostility was focused on the collaborators of

Jewish descent, rather than on the many non-Jews who staffed the new regime. The Jews who tossed in their lot with the new regime quickly recognized that they had to rely entirely on the Soviets not only for their positions but for their very lives. Whether out of necessity or design, Stalin had created a class of people wholly dependent on him, hence extraordinarily pliable. It was partly for this reason that, while Stalin launched an anti-Semitic campaign inside the Soviet Union in 1948, in eastern Europe he maintained his support for his Jewish pawns, at least for a few years. His motives for doing so were linked to the specter of Titoism that gripped the Kremlin in the late 1940's: the Communists of Jewish origin seemed the least likely to form an alliance with the local populace against the hegemony of the Soviets.

In the early 1950s, however, the Titoist scare passed, and the Soviets were in a position to sacrifice their eastern European Jewish pawns. In an attempt to broaden their own popular support, even some local Communist leaders of Jewish origin tried to use the Soviet-generated renewal of anti-Semitism for their own purposes. Ultimately, it was far more potent as a weapon when turned against them.

Hungary after World War II

The pattern common to eastern Europe mani-
fested itself with particular force in Hungary.
Nowhere were Jews more prominent in the
Sovietization of the nation. At the core of the
process was the handful of Muscovites who had
spent years and even decades in the Soviet
Union. During the interwar period the Hungarian Communist party had been banned and
unpopular; its membership was tiny; and its
leadership was disproportionately Jewish. In
postwar Hungary, the key post of general secretary was once again occupied by a Jew,
Mátyás Rákosi.

A veteran Communist who, as we have seen,
had been active in the Hungarian Soviet Republic of 1919, Rákosi was subsequently be-
trayed by a fellow Communist and imprisoned
for years by the Horthy regime. Traded to the
Soviet Union in 1940, Rákosi spent the war
years in Moscow and learned the requisite
skills for survival in Stalinist Russia. He billed
himself as "Stalin's best pupil," and was at the
side of the "sun of the peoples" during the cel-
ebrations marking the dictator's seventieth
birthday in 1949. It was this pupil of Stalin who
coined the term "salami tactics" to describe the

way in which the Communists with the backing of the Red Army sliced away all competing parties on their path to exclusive control.

The next three major slots in the Communist hierarchy were also filled by men of Jewish birth. Ernö Gerö (Singer), a Muscovite and veteran of the Spanish Civil War, became minister of state; Mihály Farkas (Wolf), another Muscovite, became minister of defense; and József Révai was the party's chief ideologist and minister of culture. The chief of the Hungarian economy was Zoltán Vas (Weinberger), also of Jewish origin and a Muscovite.

As was the case in every other country, only a minority of Hungarian Jews were Communists. Obviously, those who valued their Jewishness the most were the least inclined toward the party, and many Hungarian Jews feared that it was they who would pay for the popular hatred of the regime. Yet the core of Muscovites was also joined by a larger number of Hungarian Jews. Some, who had returned from concentration camps or who survived the war in Budapest, owed to the Soviets their escape from death at the hands of the Nazis and their Hungarian collaborators, the Arrow Cross. For them, at least, the Soviets were "liberators," even if few of their countrymen regarded them as such, and the Red Army remained the only real guarantor of their safety. Alongside this motive of physical preservation there was among some young Jews a burning desire for vengeance against the Hungarians who had murdered their families or aided the Germans in doing so. These young men and women joined the new Soviet-dominated security apparatus, for which they were suited by their knowledge of Hungarian conditions and their allegiance to the Soviet cause. It is estimated that 30 percent or more of higher police officials in the postwar years were of Jewish origin, and many departments of the security apparatus were headed by Jews. At the pinnacle of the Hungarian political police, the AVO, was a Jew, Major General Gábor Péter (born Benö Auspitz). By moving into the army, the police, and the security apparatus, these young Jewish survivors put themselves in a position to settle accounts with the men of the Arrow Cross.

The attractions of Marxist ideology also drew some of the more idealistic young Jewish survivors. The universalism of Marxism, its promise to end all distinctions based upon ethnic or religious origin, was almost irresistible to some young Jews who could recall only the irredentist nationalism of the interwar era, the growth of Hungarian fascism and official anti-Semitism, the deadly "labor battalions" into which the Horthy regime had consigned all Jewish males from sixteen to sixty-five, and finally the systematic murder of the Jews under German auspices but with Hungarian collaboration.

Other Jews who decided to remain in Hungary reconciled themselves to the inevitability of Soviet domination and hoped to make the best of it. Though the socialization measures of the Communist regime destroyed the remnants of the Jewish commercial middle class, some Jews continued to play an important economic role in Hungarian life as heads of newly nationalized industries. And though university admissions were now to favor the offspring of workers and peasants, young Jews active in the Communist party were permitted to enroll.

Hungary was a country with a small educated elite. Because in Soviet eyes most educated non-Jews were tainted by their ties to the former regime, Jews were catapulted into positions of authority. For a brief moment after the war, Jews seemed to become a privileged class in Hungary. Suddenly, reality seemed to bear out the old stereotype identifying Jews as such with Communism. As a contemporary joke had it, if a factory employed three Jews, one was the manager, a second the accountant, and the third the secretary of the party cell. For those so inclined, it was easier than ever to believe that all Jews were Communists, and since Jews were apparently in prominent positions everywhere, it was even possible to give credence to the anti-Semitic claim that more Jews had returned from the concentration camps than had been deported in 1944. The recrudescence of anti-Semitism erupted in two anti-Jewish riots during the summer of 1946. The fact that the rioters included some Communists was covered up by the local Communist commander, who was himself Jewish.

The Communists' favorable attitude toward the offspring of Jewish victims of fascism began to change in late 1947, when Rákosi decided to end the admission of Jews to official posts. After the elimination of all competing parties in 1948, there followed an era of increasing anti-Jewish repression, initiated and headed by men who were themselves of Jewish origin. In 1949 the representative of the American Jewish Joint Relief Organization in Budapest was arrested and expelled. A ban was placed on Zionist activity, and Hungarian Zionist leaders were imprisoned and forced to appear in show trials. The security services set up a division to deal with Zionism; it was headed by Major János Komlós, who at one time had been a student in the Budapest rabbinical seminary.

Like their counterparts throughout eastern Europe, the leaders of the Hungarian Communist party set out to emulate the purported successes of the Soviet path of economic development and began a program of rapid industrialization and collectivization of agriculture. As in the Soviet case, the growth of heavy industry was to occur at the expense of the agricultural and consumer sectors—that is, through the increased exploitation of the workers and peasants. The result was a decline of living standards for most Hungarians, coupled with increased governmental repression to prevent protest and revolt. Soon the prisons were filled, and forced-labor camps sprang up around the country, especially near mining and industrial centers. From 1952 through 1955 the police opened files on over a million Hungarians, 45 percent of whom were penalized. In four years, 7 percent of Hungarians over the age of eighteen were convicted and punished.

Together with increased repression went the purge of the party. Most of the members of the erstwhile Communist underground who had remained in Hungary during the war were purged as potential "Titoists," including László Rajk, who was tried and executed on trumped-up charges in 1949. In a few years, the Communist regime of Rákosi killed more Communists than had the anti-Communist regime of Admiral Horthy.

Jews were very salient in the apparatus of repression, including Mihaly Farkas, the minister of defense and chief of internal security, and Gábor Péter of the AVO. Many of Péter's immediate deputies were also Jews who had been trained by the Soviets at the Dzerzhinsky Institute in the USSR. As this apparatus of repression expanded, it recruited those with the most experience at brutal methods of interrogation, namely, former Horthyites and members of the Arrow Cross. Thus former Jewish victims of fascism and former fascists worked side by side in the creation of a Communist Hungary.

The next act in the drama of Hungarian Jewry was more absurd still. Late in 1952, "Stalin's brightest pupil" learned of the plans for the upcoming "Doctors' Trial" in the homeland of socialism, in which seven of the nine defendants were to be Jews, and in which anti-Semitic themes were to be more blatant than ever. Fearing for their own necks, Rákosi and the Hungarian leadership initiated their own anti-Semitic crusade. The head of the Jewish community, Lajos Stöckler, was arrested. So was the chief of the former Jewish Hospital, László Benedek (though he was a loyal Communist), and a number of Jewish doctors. Like their counterparts in Moscow, the Hungarian Jewish physicians were to be charged with medical crimes. The leaders of the Jewish central committee of social affairs, the brothers Szücs, were driven to suicide in this campaign, while the Jewish Muscovites rewrote their biographies and recast their style of life to appear more Magyar than the Magyars. Rákosi's official biography now claimed he was descended from the lower Magyar gentry; at the same time, Rákosi spread the false rumor that his leading rival within the party leadership, Imre Nagy, was a Jew.

There now began a clear policy of eliminating Jews from positions of leadership and from the lower cadres of the party. Vas, the chairman of central planning, was purged. Jews were eliminated as officers of the police and the AVO; in January 1953, Gábor Péter himself was imprisoned. Plans were made for an anti-cosmopolitan, anti-Zionist show trial, at which Péter would be a star defendant. Only the death of Stalin prevented the anti-Semitic trial, which would have been presided over by Jewish Communists.

The end of the Titoist specter and the revolt of the East Berliners against Soviet domination in June 1953 gave Stalin's successors second thoughts about Soviet policy in eastern Europe. Rákosi was summoned to Moscow and chastised before the Presidium, though he had merely carried out faithfully the policy of his Russian model, including the cult of personality. Beria addressed Rákosi in words that echoed the Tharauds' *Quand Israël est roi* of three decades before: "We know that there have been in Hungary, apart from its own rulers, Turkish sultans, Austrian emperors, Tartar khans, and Polish princes. But, as far as we know, Hungary has never had a Jewish king. Apparently this is what you have become. Well, you can be sure we won't allow it."

Rákosi was replaced as premier by the non-Jewish Imre Nagy. But the Soviets, who considered Rákosi and Gerö the most slavishly reliable of the Hungarian Communists, soon put Rákosi back in the saddle (in April 1955). Rákosi then had Nagy expelled from the party. On both sides of the struggle between the Stalinists and the more reformist Communists around Nagy, Jews were well represented. As the threat of popular revolution grew in Hungary, the Soviet leadership reluctantly decided to sacrifice the Jewish Muscovites. In July 1956, Rákosi was removed from office by the Soviets and spirited away to Moscow in disgrace. His successor, Gerö, proved no more popular but less crafty; in October, with revolution under way in the streets of Budapest, it was his turn for the flight to Moscow, as the Russians offered their support to Nagy.

When the spontaneous revolution threatened the overthrow of the Communist regime, even non-Communist Hungarian Jews (especially outside the capital) came to fear for their lives, on the grounds that Jews as such were identified with Communism in the public mind. During the "Hungarian October" and its aftermath, over 20,000 of the 120,000 Jews remaining in Hungary departed for the West. In November, Nagy's bold attempt to form a multiparty government and withdraw from the Warsaw Pact led to Soviet intervention and the brutal repression of the Hungarian revolution. Janos Kádár, a Communist who had himself been tortured by the secret police during the Rákosi era, was installed by the Soviets as their new man in Budapest. Desperate for public support, some members of the Kádár regime tried to "play the national card." One of Kádár's ministers, György Márosan—whose wife was of Jewish origin—emphasized in his speeches that the new leadership was not made up of Jews. Many of the Jews who remained in Hungary, afraid that popular loathing of the former Muscovite leadership would result in an outbreak of overt anti-Semitism, rallied to Kádár nevertheless. While he was in power, Jews were not excluded from positions of prestige and responsibility.

Elsewhere in the Soviet Bloc

Events elsewhere in the postwar Soviet bloc followed a similar pattern, often with more disastrous results for the Jews. The consolidation of Communist hegemony under Muscovite leadership was regularly followed by the subversion of the organized Jewish community, with Zionists singled out for especially harsh treatment. As the masses increasingly showed themselves ready to engage in open revolt against the hated system imposed by the USSR, the Soviets everywhere tried to sacrifice the Jewish Muscovites and replace them with less unpopular "native" Communist leaders. These in turn often found it convenient to divert anti-Communist sentiment into the channels of anti-Semitism.

In Czechoslovakia, where the Communists established their dictatorship in 1948, the general secretary of the party was Rudolf Slansky, a veteran Communist of Jewish origin, and a Muscovite. With Communist hegemony secure, a purge aimed at non-Moscow Commu-

nists was set in motion in 1950. Jews were conspicuous objects of a second wave of purges in
1951, which included among its victims the
deputy general secretary of the party, Josef
Frank, and Jewish deputy ministers of foreign
affairs, foreign trade, and finance. Finally, in
November 1951, Slansky—who less than two
years earlier had offered the official tribute to
Stalin on the occasion of the latter's seventieth
birthday—was arrested. Slansky became the
focus of the most infamous show trial of the
postwar era, organized with the close cooperation of agents of the Soviet ministry of state
security. Of the fourteen leading party members placed on trial for crimes against the state
in 1952, twelve were Jews. In the official indict-
ment, their names were followed by the words
of Jewish origin. The charges against them included "Zionism," "Titoism," "Trotskyism,"
and collaboration with "Western imperialist
espionage." All of the defendants were convicted, and eleven were sentenced to death.

All this happened in a country where most
Jews had reacted to the coming of Communism by getting up and going. By 1950, three-
quarters the Jews of Czechoslovakia had
emigrated, leaving fewer than 20,000, or one-
fifteenth of 1 percent of the population. Just as
this did not prevent Slansky and the others

from being tried and convicted as Jews, it did not prevent the Czech government from launching a vehement anti-Zionist campaign in 1968.

In Romania, the old Muscovite leadership in which minorities in general and Jews in particular loomed so large was replaced in a deliberate policy of "Romanianization." The process began with the purge of Ana Pauker in 1952, and continued under her party rival, Gheorghe Gheorghiu-Dej. As would occur elsewhere, the newly acknowledged "excesses" of Stalinism were blamed on the Jewish Muscovites, such as Pauker, though she had in fact opposed some of the most oppressive polices, such as forced collectivization of agriculture.[20] In Romania, too, Jews did their best to depart. Of the 385,000 Jews in the country at war's end, 256,000 remained in 1949: 220,000 applied for emigration visas in the spring of 1950, though less than half were allowed to leave before emigration was cut off in late 1951.[21]

In East Germany, the process occurred in miniature and with variations.[22] There were few Jews in prominent political positions or in the secret police, though there were more in the ranks of the party's propagandists and ideologists. And in Germany an open attack on Jews was less opportune. Early in 1953, Gerhard Eisler was dropped from the Office of Information. Paul Merker, a former member of the Politburo known for his philo-Semitism, was arrested, and plans were made to put him on trial for his contacts with "agents of Western imperialism." Jews were arrested by the security police and imprisoned. After the announcement of the "Doctors' Plot" in *Pravda* on January 13, 1953, the leaders of the Jewish communities of East Berlin, Dresden, Erfurt, and Leipzig escaped to the West. In the weeks that followed they were joined by hundreds of other East German Jews. Stalin's death brought an end to the threat against the few Jews remaining in East Germany.

In Poland, the pattern was the same, but the results more dramatic. There the regime was headed by a Communist of Catholic origin, Boleslaw Bierut, but as we have seen, the head of the security service, Jakub Berman, the chief of the economic planning commission, Hilary Minc, and one of the party's leading ideologists, Roman Werfel, were all of Jewish origin. Minc presided over the raising of work norms and shrinkage of the standard of living entailed by the Soviet Union's demands upon the Polish economy, while Werfel toed the stultifying Zhdanovist line in the cultural realm. The pattern of Jewish overrepresentation in the party and especially in the security services made the highly unpopular regime less popular still. In 1954, on orders from the Soviet embassy, leading Jewish members of the Polish regime were demoted. After popular revolt against Stalinism reached its peak in October 1956, the Muscovite leadership was replaced by Wladyslaw Gomulka, and Berman and the other Jewish Muscovites were blamed for the "errors" of the past. Those few Jews who elected to remain in Poland—Jewish institutions had been liquidated in 1949–50, and by 1953 fewer than 40,000 Jews were left in the country—were largely purged in the anti-Semitic campaign of 1968. The last remnants of the Communist Jewish intelligentsia were dropped, to the satisfaction of the younger generation of cadres born and raised in the new Poland.

The history of Jews and Communism in central and eastern Europe deserves a fuller chronicle and more detailed analysis. Historians who have focused on the utopian ideals espoused by revolutionary Jews have diverted attention from the fact that these Communists of Jewish origin, no less than their non-Jewish counterparts, were led by their anticapitalist ideals to participate in disastrous policies and to take part in heinous crimes against Jews and non-

Jews alike. Moreover, the conspicuous role played by Jews in the Communist movement, though rarely the primary cause of anti-Jewish sentiment, fanned the flames of anti-Semitism. The prediction attributed to the chief rabbi of Moscow proved tragically prophetic: the Trotskys made the revolutions, and the Bronsteins paid the bills.

CHAPTER FOUR

THE ECONOMICS OF NATIONALISM AND THE FATE OF THE JEWS IN TWENTIETH-CENTURY EUROPE

> The whole problem of the *Jews* exists only in the
> framework of [modern] nation states, since it is
> here that their energy and higher intelligence,
> their mental capital and capital of will, accumu-
> lated from generation to generation in a long
> school of suffering, must come to predominate to
> a degree that awakens envy and hatred; as a result,
> we see an alarming increase in the literary scum
> that advocate the slaughter of the Jews, as the
> scapegoat for every possible misfortune, public as
> well as private—the more so the more nationalist
> these nations behave.
> —Nietzsche, *Human, All Too Human* I (1878),
> Aphorism 475[1]

Nationalism posed challenges—sometimes, deadly challenges—to the Jews of late nine-teenth- and twentieth-century Europe. Zion-ism arose as a response to the rise of nationalism, in two ways. National identity was by no means new to the Jews, who had long viewed themselves as both a people and a religion. But they were influenced by the ideas of modern nationalist ideology to define themselves as a nation seeking its own sovereignty.[2] More importantly, Zionism arose as a reaction to the nationalism of others, to the recognition that nationalism was bound to become more influential and would have as one of its foreseeable effects the marginalization or extrusion of Jews from the life of the nations in which they lived. There were many streams within Zionism—liberal, socialist, religious, revisionist—and they disagreed about their visions for the future Jewish polity. What they had in common was the belief that it was undesirable, indeed dangerous, for Jews to live *tachat shilton ha-goyim*, under the sovereignty of non-Jews.

In many quarters in the contemporary West, it is fashionable to assume that nationalism is a residual historical embarrassment, perhaps a massive historical mistake.[3] Partially inspired by this valuation has been a tendency among historians and social scientists to treat nationalism simply as a product of culture, often deliberately constructed by nationalist ideologists.[4] Historians and social scientists frequently invoke the concept of "imagined communities," borrowed from Benedict Anderson, to suggest that since nations are nothing but the product of imagination, they can just as easily be unimagined and superseded.[5] In such accounts of nationalism, economic factors get short shrift.

This essay offers an alternative approach, one that views nationalism as an inevitable development, deeply intertwined with many of the characteristic processes of modernity, and above all with the politics of capitalist economic transformation. Its focus is on the ideas of Ernest Gellner (1925–1995), whose works seem particularly useful in conceptualizing these processes. Though Gellner's work on nationalism is well known among academic specialists on the topic, the relevance of his work for understanding modern Jewish history remains relatively unappreciated. An explanation of the sort Gellner offers is intended to account for broad historical patterns, not for particular events, which are the outcome of local developments and contingent decisions. It cannot explain why the Holocaust occurred in Germany, rather than say Poland or Romania. (That requires additional historical analysis.) But it accounts for movements to exclude Jews from universities, from the professions, and from one or another area of economic life, movements that were ubiquitous in central and eastern Europe in the 1920s, and for government policies meant to achieve those ends that were adopted during the 1930s in Poland, Hungary, Romania, and of course in the German Reich. Gellner's theory of nationalism cannot explain the timing and intensity of political decisions to engage in the mass murder of Jews. Yet it points to deep, structural processes that shaped Jewish fate.

But Gellner, whose major contribution to the understanding of nationalism came in the 1980s, was by no means the first to provide an economic explanation of nationalism that is relevant to understanding modern Jewish history. For that we have to look back to socialist and Zionist thinkers of the late nineteenth and early twentieth centuries.

During the first decade of the twentieth century, a handful of thinkers, often of Jewish origin, provided materialist analyses of nationalism that deserve to be recovered. Most of these thinkers were Marxists. For Marx, of course, the development of capitalism was eroding national identification, indeed was weakening the hold of all particular identities beyond those of class. What counted most were relations to the means of production, whether as owners of capital or proletarian wage laborers. Many Marxists regarded appeals to national solidarity as but another form of false consciousness, through which the bourgeoisie attempted to dupe the working class and disguise the real conflict of interest at stake, namely between the owners of capital and the proletariat.

But not every Marxist concurred with this diagnosis. Particularly those Marxist intellectuals who were deeply engaged in the politics of the Habsburg and Romanov empires could not help but notice the tremendous appeal of nationalism to a variety of classes. And so they set themselves to analyzing their circumstances with the materialist tools provided by Marxism. The best known of these Marxist efforts was *The Question of Nationalities* (*Die Nationalitätenfrage*), published in 1907 by the Austrian social democrat Otto Bauer, and still cited by historians. Remarking on the book's insights in spite of its Marxist categories, Joseph Schumpeter quipped that "the skill of the analyst only serves to show up the inadequacy of the tool."[6]

Less well known to historians of nationalism is the analysis of the socialist-Zionist theorist, Dov Ber Borochov (1881–1917). Borochov began by noting that having been invited originally into societies in eastern Europe to play a distinct economic function, Jews were segregated and overrepresented in middleman roles.

In the early stages of capitalist development, as the walls of the ghetto collapsed, Jews prospered in the wider markets now open to them.[7] But as capitalist development created an indigenous middle class, Jews came to be viewed as superfluous competitors, which left them economically displaced and politically powerless—subject to expulsion, or worse.[8]

In his essay of 1905, "The National Question and the Class Struggle," Borochov suggested that over and above what Marxists called "the forces of production," that produce class conflict, there were other "conditions of production" that could generate conflicts of their own. Conditions of production included geographical, anthropological, and historical circumstances that might distinguish groups from one another.[9] Though nationalism frequently took the form of a cultural struggle—over language, customs, and mores—Borochov suggested that such spiritual slogans masked a real struggle over control of "material conditions," above all territory.[10] Just as, according to Marx, those similarly situated with regard to the *relations* of production developed a sense of class consciousness and solidarity, Borochov maintained that those similarly situated with regard to the *conditions* of production developed a sense of national consciousness and a feeling of "national kinship." That sense of national kinship was subjectively "felt by individual members as something associated with their common past." "This does not always mean they really have a long common past," Borochov noted. "Sometimes the antiquity of common past is purely fictitious." Nationalism, then, was constituted by "a feeling of kinship, created as a result of the envisioned common historical past, and rooted in the common conditions of production."[11]

Presenting a line of analysis that would later be discovered anew by Gellner, Borochov argued that far from being *traditional*, nationalism was a product of "bourgeois society," that is of capitalist development, of which it was an intrinsic part.[12]

Borochov asserted that while Marx might have been right that normal conditions of production create class conflict, the situation was different under what Borochov termed "abnormal conditions of production—when a group lacks access to land, political independence, and the freedom of language and cultural development." Under such circumstances, class conflict is abated, not because of false consciousness (i.e., a mistaking of group interest) but because "the interests of the individuals of various classes in a nation, under abnormal conditions of production, are in reality harmonious in some respect."[13] That is to say, workers and owners of one ethnic group might in fact have shared interests when faced by discrimination from other ethnic groups.

Borochov pointed out that in some cases, the interests of groups of ethnically divergent workers were genuinely different, and resulted in violent conflict. He pointed to "the attitude and behavior of the American proletariat toward the Chinese coolie," which resulted in "horrible pogroms perpetuated on Chinese workers," and to governmental restriction of immigration in the interests of the existing indigenous working class.[14] He seemed to think that such immigration restrictions would increase in the future, diminishing the opportunities for Jews to emigrate to America and elsewhere. That is precisely what occurred in the interwar period.

In one of his most trenchant formulations, Borochov wrote that Marxists who focused on the relations of production but ignored the role of geography, anthropology, and history

are not in a position to understand the national question. Therefore, the following contradictions in the capitalist economy must forever remain for them an insoluble mystery.

They cannot explain why, on the one hand, the capitalist system appears as international, destroys all boundaries between tribes and peoples, and uproots all traditions, while on the other hand, it is itself instrumental in the intensification of the inter-national struggle and heightens national self-consciousness. How is it possible that at the same time when the various societies are drawn closer together economically, and their respective and relative distinctions are modified, the national problem is intensified and various national movements develop? Unless the materialist can answer this problem, he must entangle himself in a mesh of contradictions.[15]

Borochov argued that because the Jews were an "expatriated nation," lacking land and political power, they found themselves, in places such as Russia, confronted not with individual competition but with "national competition" by policies through which the Russian state sought to place ethnic Russians in all of the economic roles performed by Jews. Once, Jews had been tolerated in order to assume economic functions left unfilled in Russian agrarian society. "But when the development of the forces of production reaches a stage wherein the native population can itself perform those

same economic functions, the foreign nationality becomes 'superfluous,' and a movement is
begun to rid the country of its 'foreigners.'
Since these 'foreigners' have no national material possessions [land or power] to use in the
competitive struggle with the native population, they are forced to yield their economic
positions, thereby losing their livelihood."[16]

Anti-Semitism, Borochov wrote, was becoming a dangerous political movement, which
flourished "because of the national competition between the Jewish and non-Jewish petty
bourgeoisie and between the Jewish and non-
Jewish proletarianized and unemployed masses."
He expected that at first Zionism would have
its greatest appeal to the Jewish petit bourgeois
and working classes, but that eventually it
would find a constituency among more bourgeois Jews as well. For the time being, they associated anti-Semitism with politically backward countries, like Russia. But contrary to
their assumptions, the development of capitalism and democracy would not bring an end to
anti-Semitism. For along with democracy and
capitalism came a heightening of ethnic competition, all of which strengthened the hostility
toward the Jews and made for a stronger and
more efficiently organized boycott against

them. For the moment (i.e., in 1905), Borochov theorized, the Jewish bourgeoisie retained
its economic position, and hence was relatively
unconcerned with the Jewish problem: "Their
personal needs remain outside the Jewish national sphere, for the conflict between their
economic interests and the conditions of production restricting economic life has not yet
reached a peak." But over time, he predicted, more effectively organized economic anti-
Semitism would undermine their material well-
being, leading them to greater Jewish national
consciousness as well.[17]

One need not endorse every element of
Borochov's analysis to see that it provides an
insightful and prescient example of a form of
historical explanation that highlights the role
of economic factors—without succumbing to
economic reductionism or to a dogmatic re-
fusal to look beyond class conflict as a motor
force in history. Indeed, we will see echoes of
Borochov in Gellner's analysis, offered eighty
years later. By then, much that Borochov could
only imagine—and much that was beyond his
imagining—had come to pass. In a sense, Gellner provides a retrospective anatomy of processes that for Borochov were an object of contemporary diagnosis and prognosis.

Ernest Gellner was one of the most stimulating social scientists of the second half of the twentieth century. Though his name is less familiar than Michel Foucault or Jürgen Habermas or Friedrich Hayek, his work is at least as broad ranging, but with the added advantage of being clearer and more accessible. (He was also a stylist of great wit, which makes his work a pleasure to read.) Drawing upon anthropology, sociology, philosophy, politics, and history, Gellner has been called "one of the last of the great central European polymath intellectuals."[18] Gellner's book *Nations and Nationalism*, first published in 1983, remains highly regarded by historians of nationalism, but the extent to which its insights help to illuminate modern Jewish history is underappreciated.[19]

This neglect is understandable but ironic. Understandable, because, on the surface at least, Gellner's book has little to do with Jews. The index to the volume lists only three entries under "Jews" and another few under "Israel"— compared to eighteen for "Islam," a topic to which Gellner devoted a number of books and essays. The neglect is ironic because in many respects the book is a product of the history of east-central European Jewry, for which it also provides an explanation. Indeed, the experience of east-central European Jewry provides the unspoken backdrop of Gellner's analysis. But so subtle is that backdrop that those who write about Gellner's thought have devoted no attention to what one might call the Jewish side of his work.

Born in 1925, Gellner was raised in a German-speaking Jewish family in Prague, where he attended an English grammar school. The family emigrated to England in 1939. During the war, Gellner enlisted in the Czech Armoured Brigade, in which capacity he returned briefly to his native city at war's end. After studying at Oxford, he went on to a variety of academic posts, first at the London School of Economics, where he taught sociology and philosophy, then, in 1984, to Cambridge, where he held the chair in social anthropology. In 1993, he returned once again to Prague to head the center for the study of nationalism at the Central European University, and it was there that he died in 1995.

Among Gellner's strengths was his ability to develop relatively simple models with which to understand broad historical processes. Indeed, one of his books, *Plough, Sword and Book* is subtitled *The Structure of Human History*. Gellner is usually classified as a structural functionalist, meaning that his focus was on social and political structures, and he tended to view ideas and beliefs with an eye to the function they played in eroding or maintaining such structures. There was also a strong tinge of historical materialism in Gellner's thought, of a variety closer to that of the Scottish Enlightenment than to Marxism. That is to say, Gellner was interested in the influence of the way things are produced on social structure, political power, and ideology. Unlike Marxists, he did not believe in the primacy of class conflict or of capital; he did not believe that capitalism was intrinsically exploitative; he did not begin with egalitarian assumptions, nor did he believe that history was leading automatically to a "harmonious universal community."[20] Gellner's was a chastened, liberal historical materialism.

Gellner's main contention in *Nations and Nationalism* was that nationalism was an inevitable concomitant of modern commercial industrial society, and that the nation-state therefore became the characteristic political form of modern industrial society.[21] In some cases, most notably that of England and France, the nation-state largely preceded the coming of industrialization. But as late as 1914, much of Europe and the contiguous regions of Russia and Asia were organized not as nation-states but as empires. There was the Habsburg empire, comprising what is now Austria, Hungary, the Czech Republic, Slovakia, and parts of Poland, Ukraine, Croatia, Bosnia, Romania, and more. Within that empire there were speakers of German, Hungarian, and over a dozen other languages. The Habsburg empire shared borders with two other empires, which were on the fringes of Europe. The Romanov empire included what is today Russia, Poland, Ukraine, and dozens of ethnic and linguistic groups, stretching into Asia. The Ottoman empire covered modern-day Turkey and parts of Romania, Bulgaria, Greece and Serbia, and extended through much of the Middle East and North Africa. Each of these empires was composed of numerous ethnic groups, but they were not "multinational" in the sense of granting equality to the many peoples that comprised their populace.

In each of these empires, the social and political structure was stratified by ethnicity. The governing monarchy and landed nobility were often different in terms of language and ethnic origin from those who conducted commerce in the towns. And those who engaged in trade were usually different in language, ethnicity, and often religion from the peasants who made up most of the population. In the Habsburg and Romanov empires, those who dominated trade and commerce were often Germans or

Jews. In the Ottoman empire, the merchants were typically Greek, Armenian, or Jewish. In each of these empires, the peasant population was itself often ethnically diverse, with, say, Polish- and Ukrainian-speakers living in separate villages in the same region.

In the nineteenth century, these societies were still largely agrarian. Most people lived as peasants in the countryside, and few of them were literate. In this sort of agrarian society, each stratum of society lived a very distinct style of life. Few people expected to move out of their inherited social positions. The children of peasants were taught to be peasant farmers. They didn't know, nor did they *aspire* to know, much about commerce or government administration. The children of urban merchants had no desire to become peasants, nor could they reasonably aspire to nobility. Nobles, in most cases, looked with disdain upon commerce: that was déclassé, the sort of thing that only Jews or Greeks or Armenians did.

In such a society, social and economic stratification was largely a matter of *ethnic* stratification. Children were educated largely by their families, and they were educated to perform the tasks typical of their ethnic group. The state had no interest in promoting homogeneity among these communities.[22] In a society with little possibility of vertical social mobility, social position was castelike; inherited social position seemed eternal and natural.[23] Until the rise of modern nationalism, all of this seemed quite unproblematic to most people.

This set of arrangements was called into question by the rise of modern ethnic nationalism. Its key precepts were that each people or nation needed its own state, and each state should be made up of a single people.

Why were the key propositions of ethnic nationalism so widely accepted? Were they the result of some intellectual error, which might have been avoided? Gellner suggests that there was a functional explanation for the rise of ethnic nationalism, that "the nation is a consequence of the functional necessities of industrial society."[24] For modern industrial society is oriented toward economic growth, and that depends on mass literacy and easy communication. Government policies oriented to spurring growth through education in a common language led to conflicts over language and differential ethnic opportunities for success.

Modern, industrial societies, Gellner argues, depend on the exchange of information to a much greater degree than earlier, agrarian societies. They depend, therefore, on near universal literacy, a standard that was simply un-

imaginable in agrarian societies. In past societies, most people learn the trade they will
occupy from their fathers and mothers. But
since modern, industrial societies are more dynamic, they depend on the possibility of training individuals for a variety of jobs. Literacy is
no longer the preserve of a specialized group; it
becomes the precondition for all economic
specialization. That means that most people
need to become literate, and require education
outside the family to be fit for work.[25] This requires standardized, universal education, and it
gives a new authority to those empowered to
provide educational credentials. "At the base of
the modern social order stands not the execu-
tioner but the professor. . . . The monopoly of
legitimate education is now more important,
more central than is the monopoly of legitimate violence."[26] A state that seeks to make its
population fit for industrialization must therefore impose education upon it. Since all parts
of the population must be able to communicate
with one another, the state must impose some
shared, common, literate culture.[27] That, of
course, is what most states—nation-states as
well as imperial states—sought to do, at various
rates, from the mid-eighteenth century on.

Under circumstances of growing literacy
and growing urbanization, the possibility of

finding a job came to depend on the language that one spoke and read. Of course, some people could and did learn second and third languages. But for most people (especially for newly educated peasants and workers), the language they knew was the only one they were likely to master. In a society based on the exchange of information, language becomes an important economic fact, for it influences the ease with which one can communicate, and with whom one can communicate. Those who speak a particular language identify with one another, as having something important in common. As, for example, Czech-speaking peasants moved into Prague, a German-speaking city, they developed a new sense of themselves as *Czechs*. In the late nineteenth century, we find struggles over the language in which commerce, industry, education, and government were to be carried out. Each group united to have these matters conducted in its own language.

There are economic stakes involved in membership in a shared, literate culture: those who have not mastered the dominant language or cultural idiom are disadvantaged.[28] But there are also psychological stakes. By creating a new and direct relationship between individuals and the government, the rise of the modern state weakened the individual's bonds to intermediate social units, such as the family, the guild, and the church. And by spurring social and geographical mobility, the market-based economy itself eroded traditional ties. The result was an emotional vacuum that was often filled by new forms of identification with the political community of the nation.[29] Thus, Gellner concludes, "Nationalism is *not* the awakening of an old, latent, dormant force, though that is how it does indeed present itself. It is in reality the consequence of a new form of social organization, based on deeply internalized, education-dependent high cultures, each protected by its own state."[30]

There is a certain dynamism and egalitarianism built into modern industrial society. For "Industrial society is the only society ever to live by and rely on sustained and perpetual growth, on an expected and continuous improvement," Gellner writes. Indeed its very legitimacy depends on its provision of economic growth: "Its favored mode of social control is universal Danegeld, buying off social aggression with material enhancement; its greatest weakness is its inability to survive any temporary reduction of the social bribery fund, and to weather the loss of legitimacy which befalls it if the cornucopia becomes temporarily jammed and the flow falters." Such a society is based on a vision of cognitive and economic growth, and in a division of labor that is both complex and changing. Since permanent barriers of rank would hamper this changing division of labor, modern society "has to be mobile whether it wishes to be so or not, because this is required by the satisfaction of its terrible and overwhelming thirst for economic growth." There is therefore a degree of egalitarianism built into the ideological structure.[31]

But there is a tension between the egalitarian promise of industrial society and its reality, especially when such a society is emerging from an ethnically stratified, imperial, agrarian past. For some groups do better than others, depending in part on what economists call "cultural capital"—on the skills, cultural traits, and know-how that an individual possesses. Those groups with accumulated experience of commerce and of literacy tended to excel, while those of peasant origin tended to remain behind. As Gellner noted, any factor that leads to differential achievement can become a focus of group identification—not only language, but also religion or ethnic ancestry.[32]

In other words, there is an economic basis for the rise of ethnic nationalism. The result was that people who had once thought of themselves as part of a clan or village began to identify themselves as members of one or another ethnic group constituted by shared language, or religion, or ancestry. When they found their group lagging behind some other ethnic group, many sought to improve their collective chances by insisting that their ethnic group should be regarded as a nation. In keeping with the tenets of nationalism, they demanded that their nation have a state of its own. In their own nation, they would be the masters: government administration, commerce, and education would be conducted in their language—and on their terms. Not every ethnic group sought status as a nation, and many sought such status without success. But when new nation-states were created in areas of mixed ethnicity, the state sought to create a homogeneous population and culture. It could do so in one of three ways: by killing, expelling, or assimilating those outside the core ethnically defined nation.[33] The third possibility— assimilation—was of course the most humane. Yet there were reasons militating against it, especially in the case of the Jews.

Gellner distinguishes between several ideal types of nationalism, all of which involve ethnicity. It is often believed that nationalism in western Europe was liberal—in that membership in the nation applied to everyone within the borders of the state, regardless of origin— but that as one moved eastward, nationalism was more defined by ethnicity. There is some truth to this, but it disguises a good deal as well. Gellner thinks it more accurate to say that at the beginning of the modern era, when modern states began to form, political boundaries and ethnolinguistic boundaries largely coincided along Europe's Atlantic coast. "Liberal nationalism," that is to say, was most apt to occur in states that already possessed a high degree of ethnic homogeneity. Countries such as England, Sweden, France, Portugal, and Spain emerged as nation-states in countries where earlier ethnic divisions had been diminished by a long history of cultural and social homogenization, including the expulsion of religious minorities.[34] The relationship of ethnicity to political structure changed as one moved eastward. In central Europe—among the German-speakers and Italian-speakers—the political structure was highly fragmented into hundreds of small polities. But in the 1860s and 1870s, this fragmentation was resolved by the creation of Italy and Germany as nation-states, so that almost all Italians lived in Italy, and the majority of Germans (but by no means all of them) lived in the German Reich. These are cases of what Gellner calls "unificatory nationalism," "in which a fully effective high culture only needs a political roof," to unite existing smaller political entities. As one moved eastward, the situation changed again. The further east one went, the more mixed was the ethnic map. There one found what Gellner calls "Eastern or Balkan nationalism," where a previously subordinate, often peasant culture was transformed into a literate, high culture, which was to provide the basis of an ethno-national state. Such aspiring nationalisms struggled "in ferocious rivalry with similar competitors, over a chaotic ethnographic map of many dialects, with ambiguous historical or linguo-genetic allegiances." The attempt to create ethnonational states under these circumstances required a great deal of cultural engineering, exchange or expulsion of population, forcible assimilation, and sometimes liquidation "in order to attain that close relation between state and culture which is the essence of nationalism."[35]

In addition to these three types of nationalism, there is a fourth, which Gellner terms "diaspora nationalism." By that he means much the same as Borochov's "expatriated nations."[36] Under this rubric Gellner mentions Greeks, Armenians, Parses, overseas Chinese, and overseas Indians. But the paradigmatic, if extreme, case, is represented by the Jews. Diaspora nationalism is a reaction to the rise of the other types of nationalism: it occurs among groups who in the earlier, ethnically segmented agrarian order had been accorded a status that combined political powerlessness with stigmatized but necessary occupations such as commerce and finance. Such groups had been tolerated at the price of political and military impotence. In addition to their tradition of alienation from the means of violence, their military weakness is intensified by their geographical dispersion, and the lack of a compact territorial base.

As Borochov had noted, and as Gellner emphasizes, under conditions of legally free competition and economic development, their previous training and orientation often make such groups perform much more successfully than their ethnic rivals[37]—more successfully not only than the children of peasants, but than the old landed and military nobility as well. For "in traditional agrarian societies ruling strata are often imbued with an ethos which values warfare, impulsive violence, authority, land-owning, conspicuous leisure and expenditure, and which spurns orderliness, time or other budgeting, trade, application, thrift, systematic effort, forethought and book learning." Yet these stigmatized traits are precisely those traditionally cultivated by the disdained commercial minority. As a result, when the legal barriers to competition come down, members of that minority do disproportionately well.[38]

But now their economic and cultural success is a source of envy, and of danger. For the occupations in which such groups excel, from commerce and finance to the free professions, are now, in theory, open to all, and coveted by all. Suddenly, the traditional nobility and the ethnically dominant majority find themselves in the economic shadow of the once despised and now envied ethnic minority. The state, which had an interest in protecting such minorities in the age of ethnically segmented agrarian empires (where they were easy to milk as a source of revenue), now finds that it has more of an interest in buying off the discontent of the wider population by dispossessing and persecuting the envied minority. This buying off has material as well as psychological elements, including the satisfaction of *ressentiment*. For such dispossession and persecution, Gellner writes, "provides a most enjoyable (except for its victims) and pathetic theatre of humiliation, inflicted on the once-envied group, to the delectation of the majority. This pleasure can be savoured by a far larger category than just the restricted group of inheritors of the positions vacated by the persecuted minority, and that too is a politically important consideration, making this course a politically attractive option for the state." "The disastrous and tragic consequences, in modern conditions, of the conjunction of economic superiority and cultural identifiability with political and military weakness, are too well known to require repetition." Though "sometimes a precarious and uneasy balance is maintained," Gellner notes, "the consequences range from genocide to expulsion."[39]

One strategy for such minorities was to attempt integration into the ethno-national majority, a strategy adopted by many individual Jews who immersed themselves in the dominant language and culture of Germany, Hungary, Poland, and elsewhere. An alternative strategy was for the minority to create a state of its own, with its own territory, government, and means of violence—the strategy pursued by the Greeks, for example. The Jews, however, had no existing territorial base on which to form a nation-state, and were thus faced with the unique and formidable task of acquiring one, along with the no less daunting challenge of transforming themselves from an economically and socially specialized stratum into the economically and socially balanced population required by a state, and outfitting themselves with the means of violence required for self-defense. They did so through the creation of peasant-soldiers, drawing upon the ideological resources of nineteenth-century socialism and populism. The *kibbutzim*, a "secular monastic order" provided "a machinery for effectively re-settling the land by people drawn from heavily urbanized and enbourgeoised [middle class] populations and effectively defending it in a military crisis with minimal and exiguous means."[40]

The Jews, then, found themselves faced with dilemmas that confronted other diasporic minorities that developed nationalist movements of their own as they came under pressure from ethnonational movements and states. They were caught between the promise of assimilation into the ethnonational majority and the reality that such acceptance was often denied them. Like other diasporic minorities, the Jews too had to transform their culture, their mentality, and their social structure if they were to acquire political sovereignty over a distinct territory, that is, to combine peoplehood and statehood. But they differed from other diasporic minorities like the Greeks or Armenians in that they had no residue of territory in which they were geographically concentrated and formed a demographic majority. Instead they were compelled to create such a center in the land of Israel (the Ottoman province and then British mandatory territory of Palestine), to which they were attached by long memory, but where they formed a minority prior to the advent of Zionism. The risks and difficulty of such a strategy were manifest, and the resulting conflict with the existing non-Jewish majority was tragic. Yet as Gellner concluded, "The problems which face a diaspora culture which does not take the nationalist option may be as grave and tragic as those which face it if it does adopt nationalism. In fact, one may say that it is the extreme peril of the assimilationist alternative which makes the adherents of the nationalist solution espouse their cause in this situation."[41]

Writing in 1961, midway between Borochov and Gellner, the German-Jewish critical theorist Max Horkheimer noted with regret,

The Zionist movement, which no longer trusts in the prospects of pluralism and the culture of the autonomous individual in Europe, constitutes the radical, yet resigned reaction of the Jews to the possibilities opened up during the past century. It is a sad aspect of the history that has since transpired—sad both for the Jews and for Europe—that Zionism was proved right.[42]

Whatever one thinks of this conclusion, it seems that Borochov and Gellner—from opposite ends of the twentieth century and from opposite sides of the watershed of the Holocaust—provide us with a compelling framework to make sense of the history of the Jews in the twentieth century. They both remind us that while there is more to nationalism than can be accounted for by economic explanations, any serious analysis must attend to its relationship to the larger economic processes of capitalist modernity.

ACKNOWLEDGMENTS

Given that this is the first of my books to focus upon Jewish history, I would like to express
my indebtedness to the teachers with whom
I studied the subject: Benjamin Ravid, Paul
Mendes-Flohr, and Paula Hyman (may they
live to 120!); and to my teachers of blessed
memory, Ben Halpern, George Mosse, and Arthur Hertzberg.

Colleagues with whom I have discussed the
topics treated in these essays in ways that led
me to new perspectives or new avenues of
inquiry include Bernard Cooperman, Jeffrey
Herf, Jonathan Karp, Derek Penslar, Aviel
Roshwald, Michael Silber, Fritz Stern, and the
late Yehoshua Arieli. I thank them all for their
advice. I am grateful to Liliane Weissberg for
sharing with me her articles on related subjects. Ferenc Katona contributed substantially
to the chapter on "Radical Anticapitalism," and
Walter Laqueur was good enough to comment
upon an early draft. The chapter on the Jewish
response to capitalism was read in various ver-
sions by Stephen Whitfield, Jonathan Karp,

and Derek Penslar, each of who contributed to its improvement. Together with Adam Teller, Jonathan and Derek organized "Jews, Commerce, and Culture," a yearlong program at the Katz Center for Advanced Judaic Studies at the University of Pennsylvania during the academic year 2008–9, and while other commitments prevented me from joining the impressive group of scholars they assembled, I profited from participating in the program's opening session and in its concluding conference.

Several of these essays owe their origin to invitations to speak at academic gatherings, and all have profited from the response of listeners in various scholarly settings. I am grateful for Paul Nolte for inviting me to speak at the conference "The Fable of the Market" in Bremen in November 2003, where "The Long Shadow of Usury," which develops themes explored in my book, *The Mind and the Market* (2002), was first presented; was first presented; to the late Murray Friedman for an invitation to the conference "Jews in American Business" at the Feinstein Center for Jewish History of Temple University in October 2004, where an early version of "The Jewish Response to Capitalism" was delivered; to Gideon Reuveni for an invitation to the conference "Jewish History

Encounters Economy," at the University of Wisconsin, Madison, in April 2005, where "The Economics of Nationalism" was first presented; and to Jürgen Kocka, who invited me to present a later version at the Seminar on Comparative European Historical Research of the Free University, Berlin, in February 2006. An earlier version of "Radical Anticapitalism" was presented to the Study Group on the Jews in Modern Europe of the Center for European Studies, Harvard University, in April 1988, and appeared in *Commentary*, August 1988. The other essays appear in print for the first time.

The impetus to revise and combine these essays into a volume came from Nicolas Berg of the Simon Dubnow Institute in Leipzig, which is publishing a somewhat different version of this volume in German translation in the institute's series, *Toldot*.

Peter Dougherty has shared my ongoing interest in placing economic matters in their widest contexts, and to making scholarship accessible to a broad readership. Our relationship, now extending over two decades, began as a commercial one but has stretched far beyond, and I am thrilled to have him as editor of this book at Princeton University Press. Daniel Chirot and Andrei Markovits served as outside readers for the Press, and provided many useful suggestions for improving the manuscript, for which I am grateful. I also thank Richard Isomaki for his conscientious copyediting of the manuscript, and Deborah Tegarden for shepherding the book through the production process.

Closer to home, I remain indebted to my colleagues in the Department of History and to the Dean of Arts and Sciences, Larry Poos, of the Catholic University of America for providing so congenial an environment in which to pursue scholarship.

My sons, Eli and Seffy, read the entire manuscript and offered incisive advice on matters of style and substance. My daughter Sara, and my son-in-law, Alan, also offered useful counsel, while taking time away from other valuable projects (dissertations and replication of our genes). My wife, Sharon, has read and commented upon virtually everything I have written, including this book, bringing to bear her conceptual, organizational, and editing prowess.

I hereby absolve my teachers, colleagues, publishers, editors, and family for any errors of fact or judgment in this book.

This book is dedicated to Steven Aschheim and Stephen Whitfield, two scholars of wit, warmth, and intellectual penetration, both of whom I met before I reached the age of twenty. Friends are rare, colleagues precious: to have had them as both friends and colleagues for over thirty-five years has been my good fortune.

NOTES

Introduction
Thinking about Jews and Capitalism

1. One notes that the excellent article "Economic History" in the *Encyclopedia Judaica*, written by Salo W. Baron and Arcadius Kahan, is tucked away in the "Supplementary Entries," as if it were an afterthought. See *Encyclopedia Judaica* (Jerusalem, 1972), 16:1266–1326. The pathbreaking article by Simon Kuznets, "Economic Structure and the Life of the Jews," in *The Jews: Their History, Culture, and Religion*, ed. Lewis Finkelstein, 3rd ed. (New York, 1960), 2:1597–1666, was not reprinted in later editions.

2. On the subject of merchant minorities see Daniel Chirot and Anthony Reid, eds., *Essential Outsiders: Chinese and Jews in the Modern Transformation of Southeast Asia and Central Europe* (Seattle, 1997); Joel Kotkin, *Tribes: How Race, Religion, and Identity Determine Success in the New Global Economy* (New York, 1994). On merchant minorities and their political vulnerability see Ernest Gellner, *Nations and Nationalism* (Ithaca, N.Y., 1983), 101–9; Yuri Slezkine, *The Jewish Century* (Princeton, N.J., 2004), 20–39. Amy Chua deals with tensions between democracy and disparate ethnic achievement in *World on Fire: How Exporting Free Market Democracy Breeds Ethnic Hatred and Global Instability* (New York, 2003), while systematically ignoring the role of culture and of human capital in ex-

plaining the success of what she terms "market-dominant minorities." There is a sensible and wide-ranging discussion in Thomas Sowell, "Are Jews Generic?" in his *Black Rednecks and White Liberals* (San Francisco, 2005), 65–110.

3. For a concise exploration of this strategy see Ezra Mendelsohn, *On Modern Jewish Politics* (New York, 1993), 16–17.

4. "The opponents of nationalism see us as uncompromising nationalists, with a nationalist God and a nationalist Torah; the nationalists see us as cosmopolitans, whose homeland is wherever we happen to be well off. Religious gentiles say that we are devoid of any faith, and the freethinkers among them say that we are orthodox and believe in all kinds of nonsense; the liberals say we are conservative and the conservatives call us liberal. Some bureaucrats and writers see us as the root of anarchy, insurrection, and revolt, and the anarchists say we are capitalists, the bearers of the biblical civilization, which is, in their view, based on slavery and parasitism." Moshe Leib Lilienblum, "The Future of Our People" (1883), in *The Zionist Idea*, ed. Arthur Hertzberg (New York, 1959), 173–77.

5. Shlomo Avineri, *The Making of Modern Zionism: The Intellectual Origins of the Jewish State* (New York, 1981), 69.

Chapter 1
The Long Shadow of Usury

1. This is the theme of Hume's essay "Of Interest," in David Hume, *Essays Moral Political, and Literary*, ed. Eugene F. Miller (Indianapolis, 1987). For Adam Smith's arguments in favor of a legal cap on interest see *An Inquiry into the Nature and Causes of the Wealth of Nations*, ed. R. H. Campbell and A. S. Skinner (Oxford, 1976), I.ix.5,

I.x.b.42–43, II.iii.26, II.iv.15. For Bentham's response see his *Defense of Usury* (1787), which includes, as Letter XIII, "To Dr. Smith, on Projects in Arts, &c." and is reprinted as appendix C to *The Correspondence of Adam Smith*, ed. Ernst Campbell Mossner and Ian Simpson Ross (Oxford, 1977), and the discussion in Ian Simpson Ross, *The Life of Adam Smith* (Oxford, 1995), 359. See also Craig Muldrew, "The "Emergence of the Concepts of Capital and Savings in the Eighteenth Century," paper delivered at the conference "The Fable of the Market," Bremen, November 2003.

2. Montesquieu, *Spirit of the Laws* (1748), part 4, book 20, chap. 1.

3. Montesquieu, *Spirit of the Laws* part 4, book 20.

4. Aristotle, *Politics*, ed. Carnes Lord (Chicago, 1984), book 1, chap. 10.

5. Benjamin Nelson, *The Idea of Usury: From Tribal Brotherhood to Universal Otherhood*, 2nd ed. (Chicago, 1969), chap. 1.

6. John W. Baldwin, *The Medieval Theories of the Just Price: Romanists, Canonists, and Theologians in the Twelfth and Thirteenth Centuries* (Philadelphia, 1959), 33–37.

7. See R. H. Tawney, *Religion and the Rise of Capitalism* (London, 1926), 36–37, for examples drawn from medieval England; Dante, *Inferno*, Cantos XI, XVII.

8. Lester K. Little, *Religious Poverty and the Profit Economy in Medieval Europe* (Ithaca, N.Y., 1978), 178–80. On the church's changing conception of usury in this period, see also Jacques Le Goff, *Your Money or Your Life: Economy and Religion in the Middle Ages* (New York, 1988).

9. Fabian Wittreck, *Geld als Instrument der Gerechtigkeit: Die Geldrechtslehre des Hl. Thomas von Aquin in ihrem interkulturellen Kontext* (Paderborn, 2002), 119ff.

10. James A. Brundage, "Usury," in *Dictionary of the*

Middle Ages, ed. Joseph R. Strayer (New York, 1989), 12:335–39; Julius Kirshner, "Raymond de Roover on Scholastic Economic Thought," in *Business, Banking, and Economic Thought in Late Medieval and Early Modern Europe*, ed. Kirshner (Chicago, 1974), 27–29; Raymond de Roover, "Money Theory Prior to Adam Smith: A Revision," in Kirshner, *Business, Banking*, 317–20. On the casuistry of usury in eighteenth-century France, see Emma Rothschild, *Economic Sentiments: Adam Smith, Condorcet, and the Enlightenment* (Cambridge, Mass., 2001), 42.

11. Quoted in Hans-Jörg Gilomen, "Wucher und Wirtschaft im Mittelalter," *Historische Zeitschrift* 250, no. 2 (1990), 265.

12. Salo W. Baron, *A Social and Religious History of the Jews*, 2nd ed., 18 vols. to date (New York, 1952–), 4:203; 9:50; Le Goff, *Your Money*, 9–10. For a useful overview of medieval Christian theological opinion on Jewish moneylending, see Léon Poliakov, *Jewish Bankers and the Holy See from the Thirteenth to the Seventeenth Century* (London, 1977), 13–35. The question of whether Jews were permitted to engage in usury was disputed within the church, on which see Gilomen, "Wucher und Wirtschaft."

13. Baron, *History of the Jews*, 11:144; Joshua Trachtenberg, *The Devil and the Jews* (New Haven, 1943), 193.

14. Baron, *History of the Jews*, 4:120–21; Little, *Religious Poverty*, 56.

15. Little, *Religious Poverty*, 57.

16. Trachtenberg, *Devil and the Jews*, 191, and R. Po-chia Hsia, "The Usurious Jew: Economic Structure and Religious Representations in Anti-Semitic Discourse," in *In and Out of the Ghetto: Jewish-Gentile Relations in Late Medieval and Early Modern Germany*, ed. R. Po-chia Hsia and Hartmut Lehman (Cambridge, 1995), 165ff.

17. Baron, *History of the Jews*, 4:202–7, 9:50ff.

18. Tawney, *Religion*, 92–95.

19. Herbert Lüthy, "Lending at Interest, or the Competence of Theology in Economic Matters," in Lüthy, *From Calvin to Rousseau: Tradition and Modernity from the Reformation to the French Revolution* (New York, 1970), 74–79; Tawney, *Religion*, 102–19.

20. Simon Schama, *The Embarrassment of Riches: An Interpretation of Dutch Culture in the Golden Age* (New York, 1987), 337, 330.

21. R. H. Helmholz, "Usury and the Medieval English Church Courts," *Speculum* 61–62 (1986), 380; Charles Kindelberger, *A Financial History of Western Europe* (London, 1984), 41.

22. Kindelberger, *Financial History*, 41–43; Helmholz, "Usury"; *Encyclical Letter of Our Holy Father by Divine Providence Pope Leo XIII on the Condition of Labor*, in Oswald von Nell-Breuning, S.J., *Reorganization of Social Economy: The Social Encyclical Developed and Explained* (New York, 1936), 367; Lüthy, "Lending at Interest"; John T. Noonan, Jr., *The Scholastic Analysis of Usury* (Cambridge, Mass., 1957), 382, a work that provides the most detailed and precise treatment of the subject, and takes it up to the 1950s.

23. Tawney, *Religion*, 152–53; Jean-Christophe Agnew, *Worlds Apart: The Market and the Theater in Anglo-American Thought, 1550–1750* (Cambridge, 1986), 121.

24. Lüthy, "Lending at Interest." On the historiography of usury see Wittreck, *Geld als Instrument*, 112 n. 175.

25. Francis Bacon, "Of Usury," in *Essays of Francis Bacon or Counsels, Civil and Moral* (London, 1627).

26. Hume, "Of Interest." See the reference to "usury" on 299. On interest theory in Hume's day see the introduction by Eugene Rotwein to his edition of Hume, *Writings on Economics* (Madison, 1970), lxvii–lxxii.

27. Bentham's essay can be found in *Jeremy Bentham's Economic Writings*, ed. Werner Stark (London, 1952), and as appendix C in *Correspondence of Adam Smith*.

28. Letter D5714, March 10, 1754, quoted in Theodore Besterman, *Voltaire*, 3rd ed. (Chicago, 1976), 350.

29. Voltaire, *La Bible enfin expliquée* (1776), in *Oeuvres Complètes*, vol. 30, quoted in Hanna Emmerich, *Das Judentum bei Voltaire* (Breslau, 1930), 142.

30. Voltaire, *Philosophical Dictionary*, translated by Theodore Besterman (London, 1972), 144. For additional references to the ancient Hebrews as usurers, see the articles "États, Gouvernements" and "Des Loix," section 1 in *Philosophical Dictionary*, 193, 281.

31. J.G.A. Pocock, *Barbarism and Religion*, vol. 2, *Narratives of Civil Government* (Cambridge, 1999), 135.

32. See the still valuable article by Isaac Eisenstein Barzilay, "The Jew in the Literature of the Enlightenment," *Jewish Social Studies* 18, no. 4 (1956), 243–61.

33. David McLellan, *Friedrich Engels* (New York, 1977), 22; on the work's importance in Marx's development, see also Terrell Carver, *Marx and Engels: The Intellectual Relationship* (Bloomington, 1983), 32, 36–38. Marx characterized it as one of the major influences on his thought in his preface to his "Economic-Philosophic Manuscripts" of 1844, *Karl Marx / Friedrich Engels Gesamtausgabe* (Berlin, 1972–) (hereafter *MEGA*), 1.2: 326.

34. Friedrich Engels, "Outlines of a Critique of Political Economy," in *Karl Marx–Friedrich Engels Collected Works*, vol. 3 (Moscow, 1975), 418; "Umrisse zu einer Kritik der Nationalökonomie," in *MEGA*, 1.3: 467.

35. Engels, "Outlines of a Critique," 418; "Umrisse zu einer Kritik," 1.3: 481.

36. Stefi Jersch-Wenzel, "Legal Status and Emancipa-

tion," in *German-Jewish History in Modern Times*, ed. Michael Meyer, vol. 2 (New York, 1997), 31.

37. Bruno Bauer, *Die Judenfrage* (Braunschweig, 1843), translated by Helen Lederer as *The Jewish Problem* (Cincinnati, 1958) and excerpted in Lawrence S. Stepelevich, *The Young Hegelians: An Anthology* (Cambridge, 1983); and Bruno Bauer, "Die Fähigkeit der heutigen Juden und Christen frei zu werden," in *Ein und zwanzig Bogen aus der Schweiz*, ed. Georg Herwegh (Zurich, 1843), 56–71. For useful discussions see Raphael Gross, *Carl Schmitt und die Juden* (Frankfurt am Main, 2000), 202–44. On Bauer's later anti-Jewish writings, see Jacob Katz, *From Prejudice to Destruction* (Cambridge, Mass., 1980), 214–18.

38. Karl Marx, "Zur Judenfrage," in *MEGA*, 1.2: 141–69. With alterations, I have used the translation by Lloyd D. Easton and Kurt H. Guddat, now in Lawrence H. Simon, *Karl Marx: Selected Writings* (Indianapolis, 1994).

39. Marx, "Theorien über den Mehrwert," in *Marx-Engels Werke* (Berlin, 1965), vol. 26, part 1, p. 364. "Nur war Mandeville natürlich unendlich kühner und ehrlicher als die philisterhafen Apologeten der bürgerlichen Gesellschaft."

40. Marx, "Theorien über den Mehrwert," 525.

41. "Der Kapitalist weiß, daß alle Waaren, wie lumpig sie immer aussehn oder wie schlecht sie immer riechen mögen, im Glauben und in der Wahrheit Geld, innerlich vernschnittne Juden sind, und zudem wunderthätige Mittel, um aus Geld mehr Geld zu machen." *Kapital, MEGA*, vol. 2, part 6, p. 172, my translation.

42. *MEGA*, vol. 2, part 6, pp. 239–40. "Das Kapital hat aber einen einzigen Lebenstrieb, den Trieb, sich zu verwerthen, Mehrwerth zu schaffen, mit seinem konstanten

Theil, den Produktionsmitteln, die größtmögliche Masse Mehrarbeit einzusaugen."

43. "Den Trieb nach Verlängerung des Arbeitstages, den Wehrwolfheißhunger für Mehrarbeit." *MEGA*, vol. 2, part 6, p. 249.

44. "Bei dem Kapitalisten jedoch erscheint der Heißhunger nach Mehrarbeit im Drang zu maßloser Verlängerung des Arbeitstags." *Capital* (Fowkes translation) 346, translation modified; *MEGA*, vol. 2, part 6, p. 243.

45. *MEGA*, vol. 2, part 6, pp. 309–10. The link between Marxism and earlier theories of usury is also noted in Bernard Semmel, *The Liberal Ideal and the Demons of Empire: Theories of Imperialism from Adam Smith to Lenin* (Baltimore, 1993), 12–13, 142–43.

46. On which see Semmel, *Liberal Ideal*, 91–96.

47. See Niall Ferguson, *The House of Rothschild: The World's Banker, 1849–1999* (New York, 1999), 260–71.

48. See on these Klaus Christian Köhnke, *Der junge Simmel im Theoriebeziehungen und sozialen Bewegungen* (Frankfurt am Main, 1996), part 3.

49. Georg Simmel, *Die Philosophie des Geldes*, vol. 6 of *Georg Simmel Gesamtausgabe*, (Frankfurt am Main, 1989), cited hereafter as *PdG* ; Georg Simmel, *The Philosophy of Money*, 2nd ed., ed. David Frisby (New York, 1990), cited hereafter as *PM*. *PdG*, 199–201; *PM*, 168–72.

50. *PdG*, 612–16; *PM*, 443–46. For an earlier formulation, Georg Simmel, "Das Geld in der modernen Kultur" (1896), in *Georg Simmel: Schriften zur Soziologie*, ed. Heinz-Jürgen Dahme and Otthein Rammstedt (Frankfurt am Main, 1983), 78–94, 90–91, translated as "Money in Modern Culture," in *Simmel on Culture*, ed. David Frisby and Mike Featherstone (London, 1997), 243–55, 252–53.

51. "Soziologie der Konkurrenz," in Simmel, *Schriften*

zur Soziologie, 177; Georg Simmel, *Conflict and the Web of Group-Affiliations* (New York, 1955), 61–62.

52. Simmel, "Das Geld in der modernen Kultur," 80–82; "Money in Modern Culture," 244–46.

53. *PdG*, 463–65; *PM*, 342–44.

54. Simmel, *PdG*, 285–91; *PM*, 221–27. On Simmel's analysis of the Jews and their relationship to the money economy see Amos Morris-Reich, "The Beautiful Jew Is a Moneylender: Money and Individuality in Simmel's Rehabilitation of the 'Jew,'" *Theory, Culture and Society* 20, no. 4 (2003), 127–42; and Freddy Raphäel, "Die Juden und das Geld nach Georg Simmel," in *Georg Simmels Philosophie des Geldes: Aufsätze und Materialien*, ed. Otthein Rammstedt (Frankfurt am Main, 2003).

55. On Weber's family background see Guenther Roth, "Weber and the Would-Be Englishman: Anglophilia and Family History," in *Weber's Protestant Ethic: Origins, Evidence, Contexts*, ed. Hartmut Lehmann and Guenther Roth (Cambridge, 1993), 83–120.

56. Max Weber, "Die Börse: I. Zweck und äußere Organisation der Börsen," in *Max Weber Gesamtausgabe*, ed. Knut Borchardt and Cornelia Meyel-Stoll, part 1, vol. 5, subvolume 1 (Tübingen, 1999), and "Die Börse: II," part 1, vol. 5, subvolume 2.

57. On France, see Herman Lebovics, *True France: The Wars over Cultural Identity, 1900–1945* (Ithaca, N.Y., 1992), chap. 1; on Germany, George L. Mosse, *The Crisis of German Ideology* (New York, 1964).

58. Weber, "Die Börse: I" and "Die Börse: II."

59. Max Weber, "Vorbemerkung," in *Gesammelte Aufsätze zur Religions-soziologie*, vol. 1 (Tübingen, 1988 = 1920 edition), 4; Max Weber, *The Protestant Ethic and the Spirit of Capitalism*, trans. Talcott Parsons (New York, 1958), 17.

60. Max Weber, "Die protestantische Ethik und der

Geist des Kapitalismus," in Weber, *Gesammelte Aufsätze zur Religions-soziolgie*, 38–42; *Protestant Ethic*, 56–57.

61. The anti-Semitic identification of Jews with plutocratic capitalism was by no means confined to Germany. For British cases see Jay P. Corrin, *G. K. Chesterton and Hilaire Belloc: The Battle against Modernity* (Athens, Ohio, 1981), and with caution, Bryan Cheyette, *Constructions of "The Jew" in English Literature and Society* (Cambridge, 1993), chap. 5.

62. Friedrich Lenger, *Werner Sombart, 1863–1941: Eine Biographie* (Munich, 1994), 210. and 452 n. 108. On Fritsch as the *Altmeister* of National Socialism, see Mosse, *Crisis of German Ideology*, 112. On the reception of Sombart's work by Jews, see Lenger, and Derek J. Penslar, *Shylock's Children: Economics and Jewish Identity in Modern Europe* (Berkeley, 2001), chap. 4.

63. On Feder's economic views see Jeffrey Herf, *Reactionary Modernism: Technology, Culture, and Politics in Weimar and the Third Reich* (Cambridge, 1984), 189–90.

64. John Maynard Keynes, *The Economic Consequences of the Peace* (New York, 1920), quoted in Robert Skidelsky, *John Maynard Keynes*, vol. 2, *The Economist as Saviour, 1920–1937* (London, 1992), 234.

65. Skidelsky, *John Maynard Keynes*, 2:236.

66. Steven Beller, *Vienna and the Jews: A Cultural History* (Cambridge, 1989).

67. Friedrich A. Hayek, *The Road to Serfdom* (Chicago, 1944), 139–40.

68. Friedrich A. Hayek, *The Constitution of Liberty* (Chicago, 1960), 81.

69. Friedrich A. Hayek, "Competition as a Discovery Procedure," (1968), reprinted in *The Essence of Hayek*, ed. Chiaki Nishiyama and Kurt R. Leube (Stanford, Calif., 1984), 263.

70. See Andrei S. Markovits, *Uncouth Nation: Why Europe Dislikes America* (Princeton, N.J., 2007), chap. 5.

71. Osama bin Laden, "Letter to America" circulated on the Internet in November 2002; "Declaration of Jihad," August 23, 1996; and tape of February 11, 2003.

Chapter 2
The Jewish Response to Capitalism

1. Milton Friedman, "Capitalism and the Jews," *Encounter*, June 1984, 74. The origin of the piece as an address to the Mont Pèlerin Society in 1972 is noted in the version published in Walter Block et al., *The Morality of the Market* (Toronto, 1985), 401. The piece is republished in *The Essence of Friedman*, ed. Kurt R. Luebe (Stanford, Calif., 1987).

2. See Paul Mendes-Flohr and Jehuda Reinharz, eds., *The Jew in the Modern World: A Documentary History*, 2nd ed. (New York, 1995), table 1, p. 702.

3. For recent literature, see Eli Lederhendler, "Classless: On the Social Status of Jews in Russia and Eastern Europe in the Late Nineteenth Century," *Comparative Studies in Social and History* 50, no. 2 (2008), 509–34, esp. 513.

4. Uriah Zevi Engelman, "Sources of Jewish Statistics," in Finkelstein, *The Jews*, 2:1520–28; and Mendes-Flohr and Reinharz, *Jew in Modern World*, 702; and Sergio Dellapergola, "Demography," in *The Oxford Handbook of Jewish Studies*, ed. Martin Goodman, Jeremy Cohen, and David Sorkin (New York, 2002), 814.

5. Ezra Mendelsohn, *Class Struggle in the Pale* (Cambridge, 1970), 1–2.

6. Yoav Peled and Gershon Shafir, "From Caste to Exclusion: The Dynamics of Modernization in the Rus-

sian Pale of Settlement," *Studies in Contemporary Jewry*, vol. 3 (New York, 1987), 98–114, 100.

7. Kuznets, "Economic Structure," 1627–30. For a visceral sense of how poor they were, see the remarkable memoir by Szloma Renglich, *When Paupers Dance: Coming of Age in Pre–World War II Poland*, trans. Zigmund Jampel (Montreal, 1988).

8. Mendelsohn, *Class Struggle*, 6.

9. Andrew Godley, "Cultural Determinants of Jewish Immigrant Entrepreneurship in the UK and USA and British and American Culture," in *Cultural Factors in Economic Growth*, ed. Mark Casson and Andrew Godley (Berlin, 2000), 133; and Kuznets, "Economic Structure," 1641.

10. Arcadius Kahan, "Economic Opportunities and Some Pilgrims' Progress: Jewish Immigrants from Eastern Europe in the United States, 1890–1914," in Kahan, *Essays in Jewish Social and Economic History* (Chicago, 1986), 107. The pattern of movement from employee to employer was already evident in the Pale of Settlement. See Mendelsohn, *Class Struggle*, 9. See also the exploration of the issue in Daniel Soyer, "Class Conscious Workers as Immigrant Entrepreneurs: The Ambiguity of Class among Eastern European Jewish Immigrants to the United States at the Turn of the Twentieth Century," *Labor History* 42, no. 1 (2001), 45–59.

11. Kahan, "Economic Opportunites," 109; and Kahan, "Jewish Life in the United States: Perspectives from Economics," in Kahan, *Essays*, 129; and Lederhendler, "Classless," 521–22.

12. Hasia R. Diner, *A Time for Gathering: The Second Migration, 1820–1880* (Baltimore, 1992), 66–73.

13. This insight stems from an as yet unpublished paper by Andrew Godley, "Jewish Entrepreneurship in America and the English Speaking World, 1880–1980,"

delivered at the conference "Jews and American Business," Temple University, October 19, 2004. See also Andrew Godley, *Jewish Immigrant Entrepreneurship in New York and London, 1880–1914* (Basingstoke, 2001).

14. Jonathan Karp, "Economic History and Jewish Modernity—Ideological versus Structural Change," *Simon Dubnow Institute Yearbook* 6 (2007), 263.

15. Jerry Z. Muller, *The Mind and the Market: Capitalism in Modern European Thought* (New York, 2002), 10–13; Baron, *History of the Jews*, 4:150–56, 170–74, 223ff; and, most recently, Michael Toch, "The Jews in Europe, 500–1050," in *The New Cambridge Medieval History*, ed. P. Fouracre, vol. 1 (Cambridge, 2005), 547–70, 872–78. A useful collection of articles on Jewish economic history is Nachum Gross, ed., *Yehudim Bekalkala* [*Jews in Economic Life*] (Jerusalem, 1985; Hebrew with English summaries). Key debates on the Jews in the medieval economy are reviewed and analyzed in Julie Lee Mell, "Religion and Economy in Pre-modern Europe: The Medieval Commercial Revolution and the Jews," Ph.D. diss., University of North Carolina, 2007.

16. David Novak, "Judaism and a Just Economy: The Question of Interest," unpublished paper, 1993, and David Novak, "Economics and Justice: A Jewish Example," in his *Jewish Social Ethics* (New York, 1992). Novak's focus is on normative texts, which should not be mistaken for historical reality. See the useful strictures by Baron and Kahan in their article "Economic History," 1292.

17. Jacob Katz, "Economic Intercourse and the Religious Factor," in his *Exclusiveness and Tolerance: Jewish-Gentile Relations in Medieval and Modern Times* (New York, 1962).

18. Derek J. Penslar, *Shylock's Children: Economics and Jewish Identity in Modern Europe* (Berkeley, 2001), 52–53.

19. Babylonian Talmud *Nedarim*, 7b; *Baba Batra*, p116a; Exodus Rabbah 31:14, cited in Jonathan Sacks, *The Dignity of Difference* (London, 2002), 98.

20. Genesis Rabbah 9:7. See Jeremy Cohen, "Original Sin as the Evil Inclination—a Polemicist's Appreciation of Human Nature," *Harvard Theological Review* 73 (1980), 495–520, which lists the literature on original sin and on *yetzer hara*.

21. Babylonian Talmud, Tractate Berachot 58a.

22. Michael Novak, *This Hemisphere of Liberty* (Washington, D.C., 1992), 64.

23. Penslar, *Shylock's Children*, 55; Baron, *History of the Jews*, 4:223ff.

24. On medieval Jewish attitudes toward commerce see the wide-ranging article by Salo Baron, "The Economic Views of Maimonides," in *Ancient and Medieval Jewish History: Essays by Salo Wittmayer Baron*, ed. Leon A. Feldman (New Brunswick, N.J., 1972), which draws out the comparison with Christianity on p. 174.

25. Victor Karady, *The Jews of Europe in the Modern Era: A Social-Historical Outline*, trans. Tim Wilkinson (Budapest, 2004), 49–52. See too Kuznets, "Economic Structure," 1607–9. Similarly, Karp, "Economic History," 249–50.

26. Karady, *Jews of Europe*, 57–59.

27. Karady, *Jews of Europe*, 62–64.

28. Kuznets, "Economic Structure," 1609; Karady, *Jews of Europe*, 76.

29. On time horizons see Sowell, "Are Jews Generic?" 98–99.

30. This paragraph owes much to Derek Penslar and Jonathan Karp.

31. Gerald Krefetz, *Jews and Money: The Myths and the Reality* (New Haven, 1982), 12.

32. See especially Edward J. Bristow, *Prostitution and*

Prejudice: The Jewish Fight against White Slavery, 1870–1939 (New York, 1983), and Robert J. Kelly, Ko-lin Chin, and Rufus Schatzberg, eds., *Handbook of Organized Crime in the United States* (New York, 1994), 295.

33. Mark A. Haller, "The Changing Structure of American Gambling in the Twentieth Century," *Journal of Social Issues* 35, no. 3 (1979), 87–114; and Henry L. Feingold, *A Time for Searching: Entering the Mainstream*, vol. 4 of *The Jewish People in America* (Baltimore, 1992), 49ff.

34. "It is a general sociological rule that all minority groups are held collectively responsible for the actions of their individual members. The measure of this collective responsibility varies with the extent to which the minority is distinguishable in appearance, and with the degree of its group-isolation" (Katz, *Exclusiveness and Tolerance*, 158).

35. Karady, *Jews of Europe*, 65.

36. Jonathan Israel, introduction to *Diasporas within a Diaspora: Jews, Crypto-Jews, and the World Maritime Empires* (Leiden, 2002), 5. On trust and Jewish networks, see also Francesca Trivellato, "Sephardic Merchants in the Early Modern Atlantic and Beyond: Toward a Comparative Historical Approach to Business Cooperation," in *Atlantic Diasporas: Jews, Conversos, and Crypto-Jews in the Age of Mercantilism, 1500–1800*, ed. Richard Kagan and Philip D. Morgan (Baltimore, 2008), 99–120.

37. Kahan, "Jewish Life," 137–38; see also Marion A. Kaplan, *The Making of the Jewish Middle Class: Women, Family, and Identity in Imperial Germany* (New York, 1991), 42ff; and Shulamit Volkov, *Germans, Jews, and Antisemites: Trials in Emancipation* (Cambridge, 2006), 210–23.

38. Kahan, "Economic Opportunities," 113.

39. Paula Hyman, *Gender and Assimilation in Modern Jewish History* (Seattle, 1995), 102–6.

40. The topic is well treated in Carmel U. Chiswick, "The Economics of American Judaism," in *The Cambridge Companion to American Judaism*, ed. Dana Evan Kaplan (Cambridge, 2005), 315–25.

41. W. D. Rubinstein, "Entrepreneurial Minorities: A Typology," 111–24, in Casson and Godley, *Cultural Factors*; see also Todd M. Endelman, *The Jews of Britain, 1656 to 2000* (Berkeley, 2002), 257ff.

42. Diner, *A Time for Gathering*, chap. 3.

43. Eli Lederhendler, "America," in *YIVO Encyclopedia of Jews in Eastern Europe*, ed. Gershon David Hundert, 2 vols. (New Haven, 2008).

44. Karady, *Jews of Europe*, 80; similarly W. D. Rubinstein, "Jews in the Economic Elites of Western Nations and Antisemitism," *Jewish Journal of Sociology* 10, nos. 1 and 2 (2000), 5–35.

45. Karady, *Jews of Europe*, 76–77.

46. I have adapted this notion from Martin Malia, *Russia under Western Eyes* (Cambridge, Mass., 1999).

47. For useful and informed comparisons of the pre-revolutionary history of Russian Jewry, see Benjamin Nathans, *Beyond the Pale: The Jewish Encounter with Late Imperial Russia* (Berkeley, 2002), 367–81.

48. Slezkine, *The Jewish Century*, a remarkable amalgam of fact, insight, style, and speculation—both founded and unfounded, 118–23.

49. Volkov, *Germans, Jews, and Antisemites*, 175.

50. On the Rothschilds, see the two-volume work by Niall Ferguson, *The Rothschilds* (New York, 1998); on Bleichröder, see Fritz Stern, *Gold and Iron* (New York, 1977); on Oppenheim, see Michael Stürmer et al, *Wägen und Wagen. Sal. Oppenheim jr. & Cie. Geschichte einer Bank und einer Familie* (Munich, 1994).

51. *Encyclopedia Judaica*, "Banking." See also Krefetz, *Jews and Money*, chap. 4.

52. Karady, *Jews of Europe*, 78–80.

53. Volkov, *Germans, Jews, and Antisemites*, 208.

54. Werner Mosse, *Jews in the German Economy: The German-Jewish Economic Elite, 1820–1935* (Oxford, 1987), cited in Rubinstein, "Jews in Economic Elites," 9–10.

55. Rubinstein, "Jews in Economic Elites," 6, 9.

56. Karady, *Jews of Europe*, 101.

57. Karady, *Jews of Europe*, 93.

58. See the chart on Krefetz, *Jews and Money*, 15.

59. Edward S. Shapiro, *A Time for Healing: American Jewry since World War II* (Baltimore, 1992), 118–20.

60. Shapiro, *A Time for Healing*, 114–16.

61. Shapiro, *A Time for Healing*, 100–101.

62. Kuznets, "Economic Structure," 1659.

63. Mendelsohn, *On Modern Jewish Politics*, 17.

64. For a sense of the limits on social and economic mobility created by the educational system of such communities, see Hella Winston, *Unchosen: The Hidden Life of Hasidic Rebels* (Boston, 2006).

65. Mendelsohn, *On Modern Jewish Politics*, 35.

66. See for example, Jacob Toury, *Die politische Orientierung der Juden in Deutschland* (Tübingen, 1966), and Martin Liepach, *Das Wahlverhalten der jüdischen Bevölkerung in der Weimarer Republik* (Tübingen, 1996).

67. On the influence of Russian origins on American Jewish socialism see Ezra Mendelsohn, "The Russian Roots of the American Jewish Labor Movement," *YIVO Annual of Jewish Social Science* 16 (1976), 150–201; on France see Paula Hyman, *From Dreyfus to Vichy: The Remaking of French Jewry, 1906–1939* (New York, 1979),

chaps. 3–5; on England, William J. Fishman, *East End Jewish Radicals* (London, 1975).

68. Mendelsohn, *On Modern Jewish Politics*, 93–103.

69. Daniel Elazar, *Community and Polity: The Organizational Dynamics of American Jewry*, rev. ed. (Philadelphia, 1995), 3, notes that "socialism as a solution to the 'Jewish problem' served only part of the Jewish immigrant population and was a temporary phenomenon on the American Jewish scene, at that, sponsored and supported by immigrant socialists for barely a generation." On the broad patterns in question, see also W. D. Rubinstein, *The Left, the Right, and the Jews* (New York, 1982), chap. 1, "The Pattern of Modern Jewish History."

70. As a sympathetic critic of the book has recently noted, "If there is a subject treated insufficiently in *World of Our Fathers*, according to the book's own terms, it is . . . upward mobility. . . . Howe does not devote attention to explaining how Jewish immigrants and their children rose more quickly than their non-Jewish contemporaries." Tony Michels, "Socialism and Writing of American Jewish History: *World of Our Fathers* Revisited," *American Jewish History* 88, no. 4 (2000), 544. Similarly, Shapiro, *A Time for Healing*, 118.

71. Jonathan Karp, "Economic History," 255, and Jonathan Karp, *The Politics of Jewish Commerce: Economic Thought and Emancipation in Europe, 1638–1848* (Cambridge, 2008), 21–37.

72. Karp, *Politics of Jewish Commerce*, 22.

73. *Menasseh ben Israel's Mission to Oliver Cromwell*, ed. Lucien Wolf (London, 1901), excerpted in Mendes-Flohr and Reinharz, *Jew in Modern World*, 10–13. On the context see Karp, *Politics of Jewish Commerce*, 32–37.

74. Moses Mendelssohn, "Response to Dohm (1782)," in Mendes-Flohr and Reinharz, *Jew in Modern World*,

44–47. The original German is in Moses Mendelssohn, *Schriften zum Judentum*, *II*, vol. 8, ed. Alexander Altmann (Stuttgartt, 1971), 3–25. On the larger context, see Karp, *Politics of Jewish Commerce*, 113–34.

75. See Adam Sutcliffe, "Can a Jew Be a *Philosophe?* Isaac de Pinto, Voltaire, and Jewish Participation in the European Enlightenment," *Jewish Social Studies* 6, no. 3 (2000), 31–51, and Richard Popkin, "Hume and Isaac de Pinto," *Texas Studies in Literature* 12 (1970–71), 417–39; Popkin, "Hume and Isaac de Pinto II,' in *Hume and the Enlightenment*, ed. William B. Todd (Edinburgh, 1974), 99–127; and I.J.A. Nijenhuis, "Isaac de Pinto und die Nützlichkeit von Handel und Kredit," in *Vademecum zu einem niederländischen Pionier des Denkens über die Staatsverschuldung*, ed. Arnold Heertje (Düsseldorf, 2000), 31–53.

76. Karp, *Politics of Jewish Commerce*, 202–7; and Penslar, *Shylock's Children*, 68–84.

77. Penslar, *Shylock's Children*, 144–47.

78. See the astute observations of Ernest Gellner, *Language and Solitude: Wittgenstein, Malinowski, and the Habsburg Dilemma* (Cambridge, 1998), part 1.

79. See Muller, *Mind and Market*, chap. 7, "Karl Marx: From Jewish Usury to Universal Vampirism."

80. Nicolas Berg, *Luftmenschen: Zur Geschichte einer Metapher* (Göttingen, 2008), 90–91.

81. Quoted in Leonard Dinnerstein, *Antisemitism in America* (New York, 1994), 81.

82. Penslar, *Shylock's Children* 208–9; and Berg, *Luftmenschen*, 87ff.

83. Penslar, *Shylock's Children* 208–9.

84. Berg, *Luftmenschen*, 87.

85. On Gordon and Borochov see Borochov, "Our Platform" (1906) in Hertzberg, *The Zionist Idea*, 365; Gordon, "People and Labor" (1911), in Hertzberg, *The*

Zionist Idea, 372–74; and the useful discussion of each thinker in Gideon Shimoni, *The Zionist Ideology* (Hanover, 1995), 179–89, 208–16; and also Berg, *Luftmenschen*, 93ff. For a detailed reconstruction of Borochov's political and intellectual development, see Jonathan Frankel, *Prophecy and Politics: Socialism, Nationalism, and the Russian Jews, 1862–1917* (Cambridge, 1984), chap. 7. For more on Borochov's analysis see chapter 4 of this volume, "The Economics of Nationalism and the Fate of the Jews in Twentieth-Century Europe."

86. Hasia Diner, *A New Promised Land: A History of Jews in America* (New York, 2003), 54.

87. Penslar, *Shylock's Children*, 246, and Jonathan L. Dekel-Chen, *Farming the Red Land: Jewish Agricultural Colonization and Local Soviet Power, 1924–1941* (New Haven, 2005).

88. Shimoni, *The Zionist Ideology*, 308.

89. Shimoni, *The Zionist Ideology*, 252–56; Derek J. Penslar, "Is Israel a Jewish State?" in his *Israel in History: The Jewish State in Comparative Perspective* (London, 2007), 78.

90. Gellner, *Nations and Nationalism* , 107–8.

91. Penslar, "Is Israel a Jewish State?" 79–80.

92. Kuznets, "Economic Structure," 1650–51.

93. Penslar, "Is Israel a Jewish State?" 78.

94. Serge Schmemann, "Israel Redefines Its Dream, Finding Wealth in High Tech," *New York Times*, April 18, 1998.

95. Penslar, "Is Israel a Jewish State?" 78; and Penslar, *Shylock's Children*, 258–59.

96. Seymour Martin Lipset and Earl Raab, *Jews and the New American Scene* (Cambridge, Mass., 1995), 160.

97. Friedman, "Capitalism and the Jews," 79.

98. "In Navaredok [the fanatically moralistic *yeshiva* at the center of Grade's novel], no one was held in greater contempt than a shopkeeper. A shopkeeper couldn't be truly good even if he crawled out of his skin. His god was a kopeck, and he also wheeled and dealed with the Master of the Universe." Chaim Grade, *The Yeshiva*, 2 vols. (Indianapolis, 1976), 59. On the snares of affluence as a theme in postwar American Jewish sermons, see the dissertation in progress at New York University by Rachel Kranson, *Grappling with the Good Life: Anxieties of Jewish Affluence in Postwar America, 1945–1967*, a portion of which was presented at the Association for Jewish Studies conference, December 2008.

99. See the comments by newspapers in antebellum Buffalo, New York, contrasting Jewish immigrants favorably with the Irish, in David A. Gerber, "Elite Anti-Semitism in the Marketplace," in *Anti-Semitism in American History*, ed. Gerber (Urbana, 1986), 210; and the positive side of the evaluation of the Jew as "economic man" in American public opinion, discussed in Charles Herbert Stember et al., *Jews in the Mind of America* (New York, 1966), 57, 386–87, and passim; and more generally Oscar Handlin, "American Views of the Jew at the Opening of the Twentieth Century," *Publications of the American Jewish Historical Society* 40 (1951): 320–44.

100. See Muller, *Mind and Market*, chaps. 11 and 13.

101. See on this theme Chua, *World on Fire*; and Penslar, *Shylock's Children*, 134; and Slezkine, *The Jewish Century*.

102. Sowell, "Are Jews Generic?" 76–77.

103. On Jews in German philanthropy see Werner Mosse, *The German-Jewish Economic Elite, 1820–1935: A Sociocultural Profile* (London, 1989), chap. 10.

Chapter 3
Radical Anticapitalism

1. I wish to thank Ferenc Katona for his assistance in research in Hungarian sources for this essay.

On Jews and Communism, I have drawn on R. V. Burks, *The Dynamics of Communism in Eastern Europe* (Princeton, 1961); François Fejtö, *Les Juifs et l'Antisemitisme dans les Pays Coummunistes* (Paris, 1960), Paul Lendvai, *Anti-Semitism in Eastern Europe* (London, 1971); Branko Lazitch, *Biographical Dictionary of the Comintern*, rev. ed. (Stanford, Calif., 1986); Walter Z. Laqueur, "Revolution-ism and the Jews," *Commentary*, February 1971; Jacob L. Talmon, "Jews between Revolution and Counter-Revolution," in his *Israel among the Nations* (London, 1970), and "Jews and Revolution" (in Hebrew) in Talmon, *Be-edan Ha-alimut* (Tel Aviv, 1975); Ezra Mendelsohn, *The Jews of East Central Europe between the Wars* (Bloomington, 1983); Mendelsohn, *On Modern Jewish Politics*, chap. 4; Robert Wistrich, *Revolutionary Jews from Marx to Trotsky* (London, 1976) and Wistrich, *Socialism and the Jews: The Dilemmas of Assimilation in Germany and Austria-Hungary* (Rutherford, N.J., 1982). There is an excellent collection of recent scholarship, Dan Diner and Jonathan Frankel, eds., *Dark Times, Dire Decisions: Jews and Communism* (New York, 2004).

2. On Egypt, see Walter Laqueur's portrait of Henri Curiel in *Dying for Jerusalem* (Naperville, Ill., 2006); on Joe Slovo, and Rusty and Hilda Bernstein of South Africa see Glenn Frankel, *Rivonia's Children: Three Families and the Cost of Conscience in White South Africa* (New York, 1999).

3. See Mendelsohn, *On Modern Jewish Politics*, 98–100, and Slezkine, *The Jewish Century*, 152–53. Slezkine's book

is reliable and incisive in dealing with the assimilated Russian-speaking Jews of the Soviet Union, but becomes ever less reliable when it deals with the remainder of the Jews of the Soviet Union, the United States, and the land of Israel.

4. On Russia and Ukraine see Arthur E. Adams, *Bolsheviks in the Ukraine* (New Haven, 1963); Robert Conquest, *Harvest of Sorrow: Soviet Collectivization and the Terror Famine* (New York, 1986); Otto Heller, *Der Untergang des Judentums*, 2nd ed. (Berlin, 1933), esp. 230–35; Taras Hunczak, ed., *The Ukraine, 1917–1921: A Study in Revolution* (Cambridge, Mass., 1977); Stuart Kahan, *The Wolf of the Kremlin* (New York, 1987); Joseph Nedava, *Trotsky and the Jews* (Philadelphia, 1972); Hans Rogger, *Jewish Policies and Right-Wing Politics in Imperial Russia* (Berkeley, 1986); Leonard B. Schapiro, "The Role of the Jews in the Russian Revolutionary Movement," in his *Russian Studies* (New York, 1987); Zvi Y. Gitelman, *A Century of Ambivalence: The Jews of Russia and the Soviet Union, 1881 to the Present*, 2nd ed. (Bloomington, 2001).

5. On Jewish social, economic, and educational mobility in the early Soviet period see Slezkine, *The Jewish Century*, 216ff.

6. Johannes Rogalla von Bieberstein, *Jüdischer Bolshewismus: Mythos und Realität* (Schellroda, 2003), chap. 5. Despite its tendentious suggestion that Jews as a whole are as guilty of Communism as Germans are of Nazism, this work contains a wealth of information. Slezkine too notes that "foreign service was an almost exclusively Jewish specialty" (*The Jewish Century*, 255). See too Annie Kriegel and Stephane Courtois, *Eugen Fried: Le grand secret du PCF* (Paris, 1997).

7. Gitelman, *A Century of Ambivalence*, 112.

8. Slezkine, *The Jewish Century*, 275.

9. Slezkine, *The Jewish Century*, 301ff.

10. On German Jews and their politics see Toury, *Die politischen Orientierung der Juden*; Donald L. Niewyk, *The Jews in Weimar Germany* (Bloomington, 1980).

11. See Niewyk, *Jews in Weimar Germany*, and Werner Agnress, "Juden im politischen Leben der Revolutionszeit," in *Deutsches Judentum im Krieg und Revolution, 1916–1923*, ed. Werner Mosse (Tübingen, 1971).

12. See Rudolf Tokes, *Bela Kun and the Hungarian Soviet Republic* (New York, 1967); Frank Eckelt, "The Internal Policies of the Hungarian Soviet Republic," in *Hungary in Revolution, 1918–19*, ed. Ivan Volgyes (Lincoln, Nebr., 1971); William O. McCagg, "Jews in Revolutions: The Hungarian Experience," *Journal of Social History* 28 (1972), 78–105.

13. See the bills reproduced and analyzed in Liliane Weissberg, "Antisemitische Motive und Texte auf dem Notgeld der 20er Jahre," in *Abgestempelt. Judenfeindliche Postkarten. auf der Grundlage der Sammlung Wolfgang Haney*, ed. Helmut Gold und Georg Heuberger (Frankfurt am Main, 1999).

14. Feingold, *A Time for Searching*, 6–8, 223–24; Dinnerstein, *Anti-Semitism in America*, 79–80, 95–96. See also Joseph W. Bendersky, *The Jewish Threat: Anti-Semitic Politics in the U.S. Army* (New York, 2000).

15. See Mendelsohn, *Jews of East Central Europe*; on Poland see also Jaff Schatz, *The Generation: The Rise and Fall of the Jewish Communists of Poland* (Berkeley, 1991). On Romania, Stephen Fischer-Galati, "Fascism, Communism and the Jewish Question in Romania," in *Jews and Non-Jews in Eastern Europe, 1918–1945*, ed. Bela Vago and George Mosse (Jerusalem, 1974); Vladimir Tismaneanu, *Stalinism for All Seasons: A Political History of Romanian Communism* (Berkeley, 2003).

16. For figures on Romania, Robert Levy, *Anna Pauker: The Rise and Fall of a Jewish Communist* (Berkeley, 2001), 5.

17. Dan Diner and Jonathan Frankel, "Introduction—Jews and Communism: The Utopian Temptation," in Diner and Frankel, *Dark Times, Dire Decisions*, 8.

18. On Poland, see Schatz, *The Generation*; and Josef Banas, *The Scapegoats: The Exodus of the Remnants of Polish Jewry* (New York, 1979), Michael Borwicz, "Polish-Jewish Relations, 1944–1947," in *The Jews in Poland*, ed. Chimen Abramsky et al. (Oxford, 1986), Michael Chechinski, *Poland: Communism, Nationalism, Anti-Semitism* (New York, 1982), Marx Hillel, *Le massacre des survivants en Pologne 1945–1947* (Paris, 1985) and Teresa Toranska, *"Them": Stalin's Polish Puppets* (New York, 1987); on Romania, Ghita Ionescu, *Communism in Rumania, 1944–1962* (London, 1964), and Tismaneanu, *Stalinism for all Seasons*; and, most up to date, Levy, *Anna Pauker*. On Czechoslovakia, The American Jewish Committee, "The Anti-Semitic Nature of the Czechoslovak Trial (New.–Dec. 1952)," mimeographed (New York, 1952). On Hungary, George Garai, "Rakosi and the 'Anti-Zionist' Campaign of 1952–53," *Soviet Jewish Affairs* 12, no. 2 (1982), 19–36; Charles Gati, *Hungary and the Soviet Bloc* (Durham, N.C., 1986), chap. 4; Victor Karady, "Post-Holocaust Hungarian Jewry, 1945–1948," in *Studies in Contemporary Jewry*, vol. 3 (New York, 1987).

19. See, for example, Levy, *Anna Pauker*, on this issue.

20. Levy, *Anna Pauker*, 129.

21. Levy, *Anna Pauker*, 173–76.

22. On the Jews in the East German Communist regime see Karin Hartewig, *Zurückgekehrt: Die Geschichte der jüdischen Kommunisten in der DDR* (Cologne, 2000), and the useful review article by Peter Monteath, "The

German Democratic Republic and the Jews," *German History* 22, no. 3 (2004), 448–68; also Paul O'Doherty, "The GDR in the Context of Stalinist Show Trials and Anti-Semitism in Eastern Europe 1948–54," *German History* 10, no. 3 (1992), 302–17.

Chapter 4
The Economics of Nationalism and the Fate of the Jews in Twentieth-Century Europe

1. My translation.

2. On the ancient Jewish origins of nationalism (along with its distinction from more modern conceptions), see the excellent discussion in Aviel Roshwald, *The Endurance of Nationalism* (Cambridge, 2006), 14–22. Salo Wittmayer Baron, *Modern Nationalism and Religion* (New York, 1947), chap. 7, contains a still valuable exploration of nation and religion in Jewish history.

3. See for example, Tony Judt, "Israel: An Alternative," *New York Review of Books*, October 23, 2003; see also the cogent rejoinders by Omer Bartov and Michael Walzer in *New York Review of Books*, December 4, 2003, and by Leon Wieseltier, "Israel, Palestine, and The Return of the Binational Fantasy: What Is Not to Be Done," *New Republic*, October 18, 2003; and by Ron Halévi, "Israel and the Question of the Nation State," *Policy Review*, April–May, 2004 (translated from the French journal *Le Debat* by Robert Howse). For a broader critique, see Jerry Z. Muller, "Us and Them: The Enduring Power of Ethnic Nationalism," *Foreign Affairs*, March–April 2008, 18–35.

4. For a good summary and partial critique of this propensity, see Roshwald, *The Endurance of Nationalism*, 8 and passim.

5. Benedict Anderson, *Imagined Communities: Reflections on the Origins and Spread of Nationalism*, 2nd ed. (London, 1991). Anderson's own view is quite different, emphasizing the role of capitalism in the creation of new means of communication that make possible new forms of identity. But that is another matter.

6. Joseph A. Schumpeter, *Capitalism, Socialism, and Democracy* (New York, 1942), 15n.

7. Dov Ber Borochov, "The National Question and the Class Struggle," (1905) in Dov Ber Borochov, *Class Struggle and the Jewish Nation: Selected Essays in Marxist Zionism*, ed. Mitchell Cohen (New Brunswick, N.J., 1984), 83.

8. Mitchell Cohen, "Introduction: Ber Borochov and Socialist Zionism," in *Class Struggle*, 13. Cohen's essay is a useful introduction to Borochov's life and thought; also particularly good is Avineri, *Making of Modern Zionism*, chap. 13. For a detailed reconstruction of Borochov's political and intellectual development, see Frankel, *Prophecy and Politics*, chap. 7.

9. Borochov, "National Question," 52.

10. Borochov, "National Question," 55.

11. Borochov, "National Question," 57.

12. Borochov, "National Question," 59.

13. Borochov, "National Question," 61, 73.

14. Borochov, "National Question," 68.

15. Borochov, "National Question," 69.

16. Borochov, "Our Platform" (1906) in *Class Struggle and the Jewish Nation*, 7.

17. Borochov, "Our Platform," 79–80.

18. By the *Financial Times*, quoted on the back cover of Ernest Gellner, *Nationalism* (New York, 1997). Gellner first dealt with the subject of nationalism in *Thought and*

Change (London, 1965), chap. 7; provided his major exposition in *Nations and Nationalism*; then refined his views in *Encounters with Nationalism* (Oxford, 1994), and in his "Reply to Critics," in *The Social Philosophy of Ernest Gellner*, ed. John A. Hall and Ian Jarvie (Amsterdam, 1996); and provided a final summing up in the posthumously published volume *Nationalism* (New York, 1997). There are also reflections on the Jewish condition in the late Habsburg era in *Language and Solitude*. For biographical material on Gellner, see the essays by John A. Hall and Ian Jarvie, "The Life and Times of Ernest Gellner" and Jiri Musil, "The Prague Roots of Ernest Gellner's Thinking," as well as Gellner's "Reply to Critics," all in *Social Philosophy of Ernest Gellner*. The volume edited by John A. Hall, *The State of the Nation: Ernest Gellner and the Theory of Nationalism* (Cambridge, 1998), further explores Gellner's work.

19. A notable exception is Yuri Slezkine's *The Jewish Century*, a work that owes rather more to Gellner than it explicitly acknowledges.

20. For his critique of Marxism, see especially "Nationalism and Marxism," in Gellner, *Encounters with Nationalism*.

21. Gellner uses the term *industrial society* or *industrialization* "in a broader sense which includes the earlier commercialization of society, which only becomes 'industrial' in a narrower sense (power machinery, large-scale production) later, thereby however allowing the social changes already initiated by commercialism to be preserved, extended and to become entrenched" ("Reply to Critics," 636).

22. Gellner, *Nations and Nationalism*, 10.

23. Gellner, *Nations and Nationalism*, 11ff.

24. Michael Lessnoff, *Ernest Gellner and Modernity* (Cardiff, 2002), 33.

25. Gellner, *Nations and Nationalism*, 27.

26. Gellner, *Nations and Nationalism*, 34.

27. Gellner, *Nations and Nationalism*, 18.

28. Gellner, "Reply to Critics," 626.

29. Gellner, *Nations and Nationalism*, 62.

30. Gellner, *Nations and Nationalism*, 14.

31. Gellner, *Nations and Nationalism*, 22–23.

32. Gellner, *Nations and Nationalism*, 63–87.

33. Gellner, *Nations and Nationalism*, 2. For a recent empirical exemplification of the processes described by Gellner (though the author fails to recognize this) see Jeremy King, *Budweisers into Czechs and Germans: A Local History of Bohemian Politics, 1848–1948* (Princeton, N.J., 2002).

34. Lessnoff, *Ernest Gellner and Modernity*, 35. The element of national definition through exclusion is the focus of Anthony W. Marx, *Faith in Nation: Exclusionary Origins of Nationalism* (New York, 2003). There is a concise discussion in Daniel Chirot, "The Retribalization of the Modern World: How the Revival of Ancient Sentiments Leads to Persisting Nationalist and Ethnic Conflicts," *Ab Imperio* 3 (2008), 1–23.

35. Gellner, *Nations and Nationalism*, 99.

36. Lessnoff's discussion omits Gellner's exploration of this variety of nationalism.

37. Gellner, *Nations and Nationalism*, 104–5.

38. Gellner, 91. For previous analyses along these lines, see the discussion of Georg Simmel and Friedrich Hayek in chapter 1 of this volume.

39. Gellner, *Nations and Nationalism*, 105–6.

40. Gellner, *Nations and Nationalism*, 106–8.

41. Gellner, *Nations and Nationalism*, 108.

42. Max Horkheimer, *Über die deutschen Juden* (Cologne, 1961), quoted in Dan Diner, *Beyond the Conceivable* (Berkeley, 2000), 201. The essay is reprinted in Max Horkheimer, *Gesammelte Schriften*, vol. 8 (Frankfurt am Main, 1985).

INDEX

Jewish economic success in, 96–97; Jewish migration from, 80–81; Jews living in eighteenth century, number and location of, 77–78; linkage between Jews and Communism in, anti-Semitism and the, 136–37 (*see also* anti-Semitism; Communism/Communists); population explosion of Jews during the nineteenth century in, 78–80; the post–World War II Soviet-sponsored regimes in, Jews and, 166–88. *See also* country names

Eckart, Dietrich, 160

economic mobility: of Jewish immigrants in the U.S., 81–82; lack of in the empires of central and eastern Europe, 203–5

"Economic Prospects for Our Grandchildren" (Keynes), 62–64

economic science: Jewish success in, 102–3; Jewish theorists of capitalism, 113–16

economic success of the Jews: across Europe from west to east, variation in, 95–100; in banking, 99; civic equality as precondition of, 94; cultural and historical factors leading to, 77, 82–93 (*see also* demography of the Jews); diaspora nationalism and, 213–14; Friedman's argument regarding, 72–73,

103; in Germany and Austria-Hungary, 98–100; higher education and, commitment to, 100–102; immigrants in the U.S., 81–82; resentment by the less successful, presence of and strategies to alleviate, 129–31; in Russia, 98, 100; in the U.S., 95–96, 101–2

education: Jewish commitment to higher, 100, 102; rise of modern industrial societies and, 205–6

egoism. *See* individualism/self-interest

Eisler, Gerhard, 169–70, 185–86

Eisler, Hanns, 170

Eisner, Kurt, 148–49, 151

emigration: from Czechoslovakia, 184; nineteenth-century Jewish, 80–82; from Romania, 185. *See also* immigration

Engels, Friedrich, 18, 33–34, 48

England, petition to readmit Jews into, 110–11, 125

Enlightenment, the: disappearance of negative connotations of usury among enlightened thinkers, 29–30; Voltaire's stigmatization of usury and Jews, 30–32

essentializing, dangers of, 76

Estate, The (Singer), 127

ethnic stratification, in the empires of central and eastern Europe, 203–5

93, 95–96, 101–2; Jewish
migration to, 80–82, 86,
119–20, 196; liberalism of,
identification of Jews with
commerce and, 127–31
Uritsky, Moisei, 139
usury: as an economic activity,
considered as, 16–17; application of the term to any
immoral economic activity,
22, 28; Catholic theolo-
gians of the Middle Ages
(the Scholastics) on, 19, 21–
23; the classical position on,
20–21; critiques of capitalism linked to stigmatization
of, 45; dilemma of religious
law and economic necessity,
the Jews as solution to, 23–
26; Engels's condemnation
of, 34; Enlightenment-era
mixed reviews regarding,
29–33; Reformation-era
stigmatization of, 26–28;
Schacher as term for, 37–38;
stigmatization, as a paradigm of, 17–18; twenty-first
century echoes of rhetoric
against, 70–71

Vas, Zoltán, 174, 180
vice, Jewish entrepreneurs in
immoral and illegal activity,
90–91
Voltaire (François-Marie
Arouet), 30–32, 41
von Mises, Ludwig, 125
Wagner, Richard, 41
wandering Jew, myth of, 158
Weber, Max: capitalism, defense of, 54–56; capitalism,

participation in a three-way
debate on, 46, 59–60; liberal nationalism of, absence
of Jews from his analysis
due to, 53–54; origins of
capitalism, explanation of,
51–53; Sombart's response
to, 58
welfare state, support of, 131
Wellstone, Paul, 126
Werfel, Roman, 186
Wolf, Markus, 169
World Bank, 70
World of Our Fathers (Howe),
109

Yagoda, Genrikh, 143

Zambrowski, Roman, 168
Zinoviev, Grigori, 139
Zionism, 106; capitalistic reality of, 121–24; economic
class and appeal of, 198–99;
labor, 119; movement away
from definition as "other"
and toward, 11–12; nationalism, as response to challenges posed by, 189–90;
pre–World War I interest
in, 146; repression of in Soviet-sponsored east Euro-
pean regimes, 177, 183–85;
as solution to the dilemma
of a diasporic minority,
216–18. *See also* Socialist
Zionism
"Zionism *versus* Bolshevism—
A Struggle for the Soul of
the Jewish People"
(Churchill), 138